UNITED METHODISTS DIVIDED

UNDERSTANDING OUR DIFFERENCES OVER HOMOSEXUALITY

DALE McCONKEY

GLOBAL PARISH
PRESS
ROME, GA

UNITED METHODISTS DIVIDED:
UNDERSTANDING OUR DIFFERENCES OVER HOMOSEXUALITY

Global Parish Press
www.Global-Parish.com

Copyright © 2018 Global Parish Press

ISBN: 978-1-7326607-0-0

Cover Design by CANDesigner
Interior Design Liliana Gonzalez by ipublicidades

BRIEF CONTENTS

DETAILED CONTENTS

CHAPTER 1
Introduction: *How Are We Divided?*

CHAPTER 2
Scripture: *Divided Over the Bible*

CHAPTER 3
Tradition: *Divided Over the Church's Past*

CHAPTER 4
Experience: *Divided Over the Spirit's Work*

CHAPTER 5
Reason: *Divided Over Evidence*

CHAPTER 6
Conclusion: *Resolving Our Divisions?*

APPENDICES

BIBLIOGRAPHY

In memory of my wife, Ingrid
In honor of my children, Kristen and Stephen
In service to my Lord and Savior, Jesus Christ

For the people called United Methodist

PREFACE

The United Methodist Church is facing the most pressing crisis of its 50-year history. At the center of the controversy is a debate over the church's stance toward homosexuality. This book aims to provide an impartial account of this controversy, a resource that will help United Methodists better understand both the issues that are dividing us and the options that are before us.

After an introductory chapter, the middle four chapters are organized around the theological sources of the Wesleyan Quadrilateral: Scripture, tradition, experience, and reason. The book concludes with a discussion of the current status of the controversy and an overview of the forthcoming special General Conference in February 2019. This overview includes a description of all three plans presented in the final report of the Commission on a Way Forward (One Church, Connectional Conference, and Traditionalist), as well as a few other prominent proposals from other groups. Each chapter is written to stand on its own, so some readers may prefer to explore the recent developments found in the final chapter before reading the Quadrilateral chapters.

Readers do not need to know any details about the organization of the United Methodist Church, nor do they need any knowledge of the terminology used to describe human sexuality. However, those who are unfamiliar with these topics may find useful details in the appendices.

United Methodists Divided is an independent project. It is not sanctioned by the United Methodist Church in any way, so readers should not treat it as an official denominational resource. At the same time, I have attempted to write a thoroughly United Methodist book. With some exceptions, I have focused my sources on books, essays, and reports written by United Methodist authors and intended for United Methodist audiences. The result is, hopefully, a thoroughly United Methodist perspective on the divisions within our denomination.

I have cited enough sources so that curious readers can locate additional details, while at the same time minimizing citations as much as possible to ensure that the book is accessible to the general reader. Of these two goals, I have given priority to the latter.

I am very grateful for the assistance that I have received from many friends and colleagues while writing this book. Chris Barbieri has provided valuable expertise for several facets of this project. Diane Land's meticulous and comprehensive editing cannot be adequately acknowledged. Maddie James and Celine Seguin furnished broad and admirable assistance as my student research assistants. My district superintendent, David Naglee, offered insightful suggestions, as did David Campbell, Scott Hughes, Jan Lawrence, Kristen McConkey, David McKenzie, Phil Schroeder, and Jim Tichenor. Stephen McConkey, Adam Roberts, and Anjie Woodworth suggested helpful design advice. Gregg and Debi Lewis shared their writing and publishing wisdom. Tiffany Steinwert made special efforts to enhance the utility of her dissertation research. Wayne Hopper preached a trilogy of sermons in my stead, gifting me with time for focused writing. This substantial assistance notwithstanding, I alone am responsible for any deficiencies of this book.

Chapter 1

INTRODUCTION: HOW ARE WE DIVIDED?

"We are and have been talking past each other for a long time.... A real conversation does not occur until each and every point of view can be taken up thoughtfully."

- Bishop Gregory V. Palmer, West Ohio Episcopal Area[1]

METHODS AND MOTIVATIONS

I have written this book to provide an impartial account of the theological conflict that divides United Methodists over the issue of homosexuality. It is not my intention to promote my own opinions but instead to fairly present the divergent perspectives that strain our denomination. However, at the beginning of each chapter I take the liberty of sharing a brief personal reflection. In this opening chapter, I would like to share my underlying motivation for writing this book.

I wear two professional hats, or rather two professional robes—the regalia of a sociology professor and the vestment of a United Methodist pastor. Of these two roles, my approach to writing this book has been more influenced by my training as a sociologist. In both my teaching and

---

1 Gregory Palmer, "Enforce," in *Finding Our Way*, eds. Rueben Job and Neil Alexander, 9.

my research, I characteristically strive for neutrality and objectivity. When instructing my students, I present them with a full range of theoretical perspectives with the reminder, "You don't need to agree with these theories, but you do need to understand them."

Similarly, I don't expect everyone to agree with the various moral and theological views presented here, but I am hopeful that this book will help readers develop a greater understanding of the issues that divide us and the dilemma that we are facing. I completely concur with Bishop Palmer's quote that opens this chapter—we in the United Methodist Church have been talking past each other for a long time. My hope and prayer is that this book helps us to have a real conversation about homosexuality.

If you are looking for solutions to our denominational crisis, this book is not for you. I propose no answers and I take no sides. My aim is to present the varying perspectives within this crisis using the convictions, language, and tone of the groups I am trying to accurately represent. My singular goal is one of increased understanding among the people called United Methodist. Wherever I have fallen short of this goal, I pray for your forbearance and God's forgiveness.

If my professor role has inspired the methods for this book, it has been my pastoral role, and more generally my identity as a United Methodist, that has provided the motivation. I love the United Methodist Church. For virtually all of my life I have been a member of this denomination, and throughout life's journey United Methodist brothers and sisters in Christ have molded and nurtured my faith. It is a humbling honor to currently serve as a local pastor in a small country church.

But my beloved denomination is in crisis. After decades of debating the proper ethical stance toward same-sex relationships, we find ourselves at a tipping point. The one thing we seem to agree upon is that we cannot continue on the same fractured path that we are now travelling. In an effort to "find a way forward" and avoid schism, the church has called an unprecedented special session of General Conference.[2] This special General Conference, set for February 23-26, 2019, will determine

---

2 There has been one other special session of General Conference, convened in 1970 to complete the formation of the United Methodist Church from the merger of the Methodist Church and the Evangelical United Brethren Church. The 2019 special session is the first General Conference called to address a crisis.

if there is a way to hold our denomination together and to remain truly united as Methodists.

This book is my modest contribution to helping United Methodists understand the reasons why we are so divided as a denomination. The issue on the surface of our discord is homosexuality, yet advocates on both sides of the controversy agree that homosexuality is just the tip of the iceberg and that below the surface lie deeper, more profound sources of division. This book is an attempt to provide a more complete view of the entire iceberg so we are better aware of the depth of our disagreement. It is my hope that this book will be useful to people of goodwill—people who truly want to listen to one another and to understand our deep-seated differences.

The book is organized into six chapters. This initial chapter provides the essential context of the crisis before us: the basic positions of the United Methodist Church toward homosexuality, the underlying source of the conflict between traditional and progressive Christians, and the theological tools at our disposal. The next four chapters are organized by the four "theological guidelines" of our denomination: Scripture, tradition, reason, and experience. Each one of these facets of our faith contributes to our denominational division over homosexuality. The final chapter provides an overview of the specific proposals put forth by the bishops, the initial responses to these proposals, and the various options before the special called General Conference that will meet in February 2019.

THE DILEMMA IN BRIEF

Since the years immediately following the formation of the United Methodist Church in 1968, the church has consistently professed a two-pronged stance toward homosexuality: (1) homosexuals are people of sacred worth, and (2) the practice of homosexuality is incompatible with Christian teaching. While other mainline Protestant denominations have softened and changed their official policies toward the marriage and ordination of LGBTQ people (Lesbian, Gay, Bisexual, Transgender, and Queer), the stance of the United Methodist Church has changed very little for five decades. If anything, the denomination's prohibitions of same-sex behavior have strengthened.

Among United Methodists, three distinct perspectives have emerged. Traditionalists believe the church has achieved the correct balance between Christian love and holiness. In contrast, progressives have been calling the church to overturn its denunciation and prohibition of homosexual practices and to become more affirming and inclusive. Between these two poles are centrists who seek to make provisions that would allow both traditionalists and progressives to follow their personal consciences on the matter of homosexuality. Over the past several decades, the tension between traditionalists and progressives has intensified. General Conferences have been interrupted by protests. Calls for a schism have grown louder. Both camps appear to be more entrenched than ever. All sides have become weary of the continued animosity, and the denomination seems to be at an impasse.

At the 2016 General Conference in Portland, delegates took the unprecedented step of asking the Council of Bishops to intervene.[3] The bishops responded by proposing to suspend further action on matters related to homosexuality to allow for the formation of a commission that would explore options on "a way forward" for the United Methodist Church. These options would then be considered at a rare, specially called session of General Conference. By a narrow vote (428-405), the delegates approved the bishops' proposal. The Commission on a Way Forward was established with a geographically and theologically diverse 32-person membership, and the special session of General Conference has been set for February 23-26, 2019, in St. Louis. It is very likely that this gathering will determine the future shape and direction of the United Methodist Church.

Although the bishops called for a cessation of any further action while the Commission on a Way Forward does its work, advocates on both sides of the controversy have been anything but quiet. After the 2016 General Conference, several of the annual conferences (the yearly gathering of regional legislative bodies) that have strong progressive leanings passed motions of non-conformity. Rather than accept the status quo until 2019, these conferences pledged to disregard any policies in the United Methodist *Book of Discipline* that they believe are discriminatory toward

---

3 This section refers to several parts of the organizational structure of the United Methodist Church. Readers unfamiliar with the organization of the church may wish to consult Appendix C.

LGBTQ persons. Other progressive-leaning annual conferences, while not passing specific motions, nevertheless took steps to disregard church policy by ordaining openly gay and lesbian clergy as well as allowing clergy to officiate same-sex marriages. Perhaps most significantly, the Western Jurisdiction (the region encompassing the 12 most western states, which includes some of the most progressive annual conferences in the church) elected clergywoman Karen Oliveto to serve as the denomination's first openly LGBTQ bishop.

On the traditionalist side of the spectrum, the South Georgia Conference passed a motion requesting that their bishop refrain from receiving or appointing any clergy who have publicly declared their intent to disregard the *Book of Discipline's* teachings and restrictions regarding human sexuality. More significantly, traditionalist leaders launched the Wesleyan Covenant Association. This new organization mobilizes like-minded United Methodist individuals and congregations to express and promote a unified, orthodox vision of Christian faith, a faith that preserves the church's historic understandings of human sexuality. Some leaders in the Wesleyan Covenant Association have publicly endorsed a formal schism with the United Methodist Church, fueling widespread speculation that this new alliance is positioning itself to separate into a new, independent denomination if they are dissatisfied with the results of the 2019 special General Conference.

In the midst of all these developments, the United Methodist Judicial Council (essentially the "Supreme Court" of the denomination) ruled that Karen Oliveto's election as bishop in the Western Jurisdiction did, indeed, violate church law because she was a self-avowed practicing homosexual. However, the Council also stated that Bishop Oliveto nevertheless remained in good standing until due process was completed. On a separate but related matter, the Judicial Council ruled that annual conferences may not ignore the sexuality of ministerial candidates pursuing ordination, thereby upholding the church's official law and admonishing the conferences that had taken positions of nonconformity.

If these developments seem confusing and chaotic, it is because they are. Traditionalists, progressives, and centrists agree that the denomination is in disarray. Some believe that our divisions are too deep and too wide to be reconciled. Others, such as prominent centrist pastor Adam Hamilton, believe that the 2019 special General Conference represents "our best chance of finding a long-term solution."[4]

CULTURAL CONFLICT IN THE UNITED STATES

The United Methodist clash over homosexuality is not occurring in a social vacuum. For the past several decades, the United States has experienced a profound division over cultural issues, challenging the bond of our shared morals, values, and convictions. The conflict has become so pronounced and adversarial that sociologists, politicians, and other pundits often describe the tension in the United States as a "culture war." This ethical battle involves a wide variety of issues such as abortion, family values, gender roles, capital punishment, and creationism. But perhaps no single issue has sparked greater animosity and division in our nation's cultural conflict than homosexuality.

At the heart of the culture war is a deep disagreement over the nature of moral authority. On one side are the traditionalists, described as conservative and orthodox, who believe that moral authority comes from a transcendent, unchanging source that is typically revealed in sacred scriptures. On the other side are progressives, also called liberal, who believe that religious and moral authority must be flexible enough to adapt to the new realities of modern society.

The extent of the cultural conflict in the United States is far-reaching, encompassing both political and religious dimensions. This can be confusing, especially because most of the aforementioned terms are used in both political and religious discourse. But when used in this book, terms such as traditionalist and progressive are used in explicitly religious terms. Thus, evangelical Christians tend to be traditionalists, looking to the past to discern and embrace timeless truths. Conversely, progressive Christians are more willing to revise conventional faith claims so they are more consistent with contemporary sensibilities. The traditionalist rallying cry can be summarized as "Jesus Christ is the same yesterday and today and forever" (Hebrews 13:8), while progressives are more likely to proclaim God's prophetic voice of change: "See, I am doing a new thing!" (Isaiah 43:19).

---

4 Heather Hahn and Sam Hodges, "GC2016 Puts Hold on Sexuality Debate."

A curious feature of America's culture war is that it doesn't fall along predictable denominational lines. People's religious affiliation tells us very little about which side of the conflict they stand. Instead, the cultural divide in the United States runs directly through most of America's religious denominations, splitting them internally into orthodox and progressive factions. Each major Christian tradition—Catholic, Baptist, Methodist, Presbyterian, Lutheran, and Episcopalian—has a sizable portion of its membership on either side of the cultural divide. This is certainly true of the United Methodist Church, and this book is an attempt to understand how United Methodists can be united in their commitment "to make disciples for Jesus Christ for the transformation of the world," and yet be so deeply divided along the fissures of the culture war.

CHANGING VIEWS OF HOMOSEXUALITY

Cultural conflict in American society is nowhere more pronounced than the battle over homosexuality. Until recently, this particular battle was relatively one-sided. In 1973, about three out of every four Americans (74%) believed that sexual relations between two adults of the same sex was "always wrong," while only one in nine (11%) believed that it was "not wrong at all." Over the ensuing four decades, attitudes have changed dramatically. By 2016, only 39% believe that homosexual relations are always wrong, and a majority of the population (52%) now say that such behavior is not wrong at all. Three important points can be gleaned from this data:

- Our country has experienced a dramatic shift in its attitudes about homosexuality, moving from being strongly opposed to same-sex relations to now being slightly supportive of it.
- The country is currently very divided on the issue of homosexuality, with 52% expressing support and 39% voicing opposition.
- There is little middle ground, as very few people believe that same-sex intimacy is "usually wrong" or "sometimes wrong." Instead, people are much more likely to believe at the poles: homosexual activity is seen either as always wrong or not wrong at all.

These same patterns can be seen when looking at national attitudes about same-sex marriage. Thirty years ago, over 70% of the nation opposed same-sex marriage and approximately 10% supported it. Since then, support has steadily grown, reaching a tipping point in 2010 when, for the first time, more people supported same-sex marriage than opposed it. In 2015, the United States Supreme Court made the historic decision to declare same-sex marriage a constitutional right, effectively legalizing it in all 50 states. Currently, two-thirds (67%) of the U.S. population supports marriage equality.[5] These national trends have amplified the conflict within the church.

Of course, not all regions of the nation believe alike. The southern and midwestern regions of the United States express the greatest disapproval of same-sex marriage, while the western and the northeastern regions express the strongest support for the right of lesbian and gay people to wed. These regional differences have an important impact on the ongoing debates in the United Methodist Church. Furthermore, the United Methodist Church is a global denomination that is growing rapidly in Africa, a region of the world that remains firmly opposed to homosexuality. The impact of these regional patterns will be addressed in Chapter 6.

OFFICIAL POSITIONS OF THE CHURCH

The United Methodist Church has been deliberating the issue of homosexuality virtually from the moment of its inception 50 years ago. As debates over homosexuality have persisted and deepened, the General Conference, the main legislative body of the denomination that meets every four years, has established six basic statements regarding same-sex behavior and LGBTQ people. These positions are found in the *Book of Discipline*, the official governing document of the United Methodist Church.[6] The six positions can be summarized as follows:

---

5   Data in this section comes from the 1973 and 2016 General Social Survey by NORC at the University of Chicago, as well as several Gallup and Pew surveys (most recently Justin McCarthy, "Two in Three Americans.")

6   Unless stated otherwise, all references to the *Book of Discipline* are denoting the 2016 edition.

1. All People Are of Sacred Worth (¶161G)
2. All People Deserve Equal Rights (¶162H)
3. Homosexuality Is Not Compatible with Christian Teaching (¶161 F, ¶161G, ¶304.3)
4. Pastors Cannot Officiate Same-Sex Weddings (¶332.6)
5. The Church Will Not Ordain Self-Avowed Practicing Homosexuals (¶304.3)
6. Church Agencies Will Not Fund Homosexual Causes (Pro- or Anti-) (¶613, ¶806.9)

Below is a closer look at each of these statements.

1. All People Are of Sacred Worth

In the section titled "Human Sexuality" (¶161G), the *Book of Discipline* states, "We affirm that sexuality is God's good gift to all persons.... We affirm that all persons are individuals of sacred worth, created in the image of God.... We affirm that God's grace is available to all.... We implore families and churches not to reject or condemn lesbian and gay members and friends. We commit ourselves to be in ministry for and with all persons."[7] Elsewhere (¶4, ¶214), the *Book of Discipline* is clear that the United Methodist Church is an inclusive body to which all people are eligible to join. There is an important qualification to these statements, a qualification that has been omitted for the moment but will be addressed momentarily.

2. All People Deserve Equal Rights

The *Book of Discipline* has a paragraph titled, "Equal Rights Regardless of Sexual Orientation" (¶162J). It states, in full:

> Certain basic human rights and civil liberties are due all persons. We are committed to supporting those rights and liberties for all persons, regardless of sexual orientation. We see a clear issue of simple justice in protecting the rightful claims where people

---

7 Appendix B provides the complete statement on human sexuality in the *Book of Discipline.*

have shared material resources, pensions, guardian relationships, mutual powers of attorney, and other such lawful claims typically attendant to contractual relationships that involve shared contributions, responsibilities, and liabilities, and equal protection before the law. Moreover, we support efforts to stop violence and other forms of coercion against all persons, regardless of sexual orientation.

One of the debates facing the United Methodist Church is whether or not same-sex marriage is a basic human right, especially now that the United States Supreme Court has legalized it throughout the United States. Progressives would emphatically say that yes, gay and lesbian couples are entitled to marry like heterosexual couples. Traditionalists would contend that the legality of same-sex marriage does not make it morally acceptable according to Christian standards. Thus, the issue for the church is less about whether or not such marriages should be legal in secular society and more a question of whether or not United Methodist pastors should be allowed officiate and sanctify such marriages.

The above two positions of the United Methodist Church—that all people have sacred worth and deserve basic rights—are the most affirming and least contentious assertions about homosexuality in the *Book of Discipline*. On these two points, traditionalists and progressives alike agree. The remaining statements are less affirming and more controversial.

3. Homosexuality Is Not Compatible with Christian Teaching

In the same paragraph as the "sacred worth" statement above (¶161G), the *Book of Discipline* also reads, "The United Methodist Church does not condone the practice of homosexuality and considers this practice incompatible with Christian teaching." In a later section (¶304.3), nearly the exact wording is used: "The practice of homosexuality is incompatible with Christian teaching." This "incompatibility clause" dates back to the denomination's earliest years when delegates voted for its adoption at the 1972 General Conference. Progressives have repeatedly attempted to overturn it, or at least to soften the wording, but every effort has been unsuccessful. It is this sentence, perhaps more than any other, that disunites the United Methodist Church.

Also in the "Human Sexuality" section of the *Book of Discipline* (¶161G), homosexuality is clearly excluded as an appropriate expression of intimacy: "We affirm that sexuality is God's good gift to all persons. We call everyone to responsible stewardship of this sacred gift. Although all persons are sexual beings whether or not they are married, sexual relations are affirmed only with the covenant of monogamous, heterosexual marriage."

4. Pastors Cannot Officiate Same-Sex Weddings

Even though same-sex marriage is now legal in the United States, United Methodist ministers are prohibited from officiating such ceremonies. Furthermore, the *Book of Discipline* forbids same-sex weddings from being celebrated in United Methodist churches. Paragraph 341.6 plainly states, "Ceremonies that celebrate homosexual unions shall not be conducted by our ministers and shall not be conducted in our churches." Much to the dismay of traditionalists, several progressive pastors have defied this policy, and recently some conferences and jurisdictions have openly declared that they will not enforce it.

5. The Church Will Not Ordain Self-Avowed Practicing Homosexuals

A perennial issue for the United Methodist Church has been the status of gay and lesbian individuals who seek to be ordained for ministry in the denomination. Under the "Qualifications for Ordination" (¶304.3), the *Book of Discipline* acknowledges that "persons set apart by the Church for ordained ministry are subject to all the frailties of the human condition and the pressures of society." Nevertheless, "They are required to maintain the highest standards of holy living in the world." According to the *Discipline*, homosexuality does not conform to such standards of holiness, and thus openly-practicing gay and lesbian members cannot seek ordination. "The practice of homosexuality is incompatible with Christian teaching. Therefore self-avowed practicing homosexuals are not to be certified as candidates, ordained as ministers, or appointed to serve in The United Methodist Church."

This issue has been a primary source of the deep fissure in the United Methodist Church. As early as 1971, openly gay pastors have fought to keep their ordination credentials. Much of the deliberation and debate has focused on the term "self-avowed practicing homosexual." The *Discipline* adds a clarifying footnote based on Judicial Council rulings: "'Self-avowed practicing homosexual' is understood to mean that a person openly acknowledges to a bishop, district superintendent, district committee of ordained ministry, board of ordained ministry, or clergy session that the person is a practicing homosexual." This has resulted in a type of "don't ask, don't tell" approach in the United Methodist Church, reminiscent of U.S. military policy in the 1990s.

The "don't ask, don't tell" policy is fading away in the church as many regional annual conferences have made public declarations that they will not comply with this official policy. Self-avowed practicing homosexuals are serving in many congregations, especially in the Northeastern and the Western Jurisdictions. In 2016, the defiance toward this policy reached a new peak when the Western Jurisdiction elected Karen Oliveto to serve as one of their bishops, the first-ever openly gay or lesbian minister to serve as a United Methodist Bishop. However, in April 2017, the denomination's Judicial Council ruled that Oliveto's same-sex marriage was tantamount to a self-avowal of being a practicing homosexual, and thus her elevation to bishop was against church law. Chapter 6 provides further details of this pivotal event.

6. Church Agencies Will Not Fund Homosexual Causes (Neither to Support or Oppose)

In two locations (¶613, ¶806.9), the *Book of Discipline* makes explicit statements that United Methodist agencies cannot use funds to promote or support the acceptance of homosexuality. At the same time, the statement rejects the use of church funds for purposes that may denounce people who are LGBTQ. It also adds the important caveat that efforts to address the HIV epidemic will not be hindered by these restrictions. The official statement reads (¶806.9):

> [The General Council on Finance and Administration] shall be responsible for ensuring that no board, agency, committee,

commission, or council shall give United Methodist funds to any gay caucus or group, or otherwise use such funds to promote the acceptance of homosexuality or violate the expressed commitment of The United Methodist Church "not to reject or condemn lesbian and gay members and friends" (¶161G). The council shall have the right to stop such expenditures. It shall not limit the Church's ministry in response to the HIV epidemic.

These six statements form the official policy of the United Methodist Church toward homosexuality, and it is the disagreement over these six statements (or, more precisely, the last four) that is threatening the unity of the denomination. Traditionalists believe these statements are an accurate statement of God's will for the United Methodist Church and an appropriate summary of how we should order our lives together. Traditionalists don't want to make the statements any stricter or condemning, but they also do not want to make them any more lenient or affirming. By contrast, progressives are fighting to change the current policies, especially the incompatibility clause, the prohibition of same-sex marriage, and the exclusion of LGBTQ individuals from ordination.

THE WESLEYAN QUADRILATERAL

The next four chapters present the many ways the United Methodist Church is divided over the issue of homosexuality. These four chapters are organized around the theological guidelines our denomination calls the Wesleyan Quadrilateral. John Wesley himself never used this term, but the Quadrilateral has nevertheless come to reflect the four principal resources Wesley used in formulating his theology: Scripture, tradition, experience, and reason. Scripture refers to the Bible, both Old and New Testaments. Tradition reflects the witness and wisdom of the history of the Church and all the faithful followers of Jesus who have gone before us. Experience is the prompting and conviction of the Holy Spirit in our personal and corporate lives. Reason acknowledges the God-given gift of our intellect. As the *Book of Discipline* states (¶105), our theological task is "grounded in Scripture, informed by Christian tradition, enlivened in personal experience, and tested by reason."

Each of these theological guidelines of the Wesleyan Quadrilateral influence and shape the debate on homosexuality, and each has been assigned its own chapter. There are some limitations of this approach to organizing the book. First, giving Scripture, tradition, experience, and reason each a separate chapter implies that all four of these sources are equally important, but United Methodist doctrine has always emphasized the central, primary role of Scripture in the life of a Christian. When people invoke the Quadrilateral, they will often be quick to note that "quadrilateral" is not the same as "equilateral." The *Book of Discipline* states, "In theological reflection, the resources of tradition, experience, and reason are integral to our study of Scripture without displacing Scripture's primacy for faith and practice."

Second, these various modes of theological inquiry are not meant to be segmented apart from one another. Rather, Scripture, tradition, experience, and reason are inseparably intertwined in one's faith formation. According to the *Book of Discipline,* "These four sources— each making distinctive contributions, yet all finally working together— guide our quest as United Methodists for a vital and appropriate Christian witness."

Third and finally, many facets of the debate over homosexuality do not fit neatly into a single category, so the placement of some topics in certain chapters may seem rather forced. It is thus advisable to think of each chapter's title as a conceptual guide rather than a hard-and-fast theological category.

THE CHALLENGE OF TERMINOLOGY

Cultural conflict includes a debate over language, and it is often difficult to even begin a civil dialogue because the terms themselves have politically and emotionally charged meanings. For example, if people of divergent opinions wish to discuss abortion, will the traditionalist position be called pro-life or anti-choice? Proponents on each side of the culture war strive to employ their preferred terms to shape the discourse to their advantage.

This battle to frame the debate is evident when considering the labels used to describe each group. Traditionalists might object to the implication that their opponents are the ones who stand for "progress," while progressives might protest the suggestion that their rivals are the rightful guardians of "tradition." Thus, it is common to find each group using disparaging labels to describe the other side, such as calling traditionalists "reactionaries" or referring to progressives as "revisionists."

Similarly, the terminology used when debating the specific issue of homosexuality can also be biased. In fact, neither side of the cultural divide is particularly fond of the word "homosexuality." For progressives, the term invokes clinical inferences that same-sex attraction is a type of psychiatric disorder. For them, terms such as "lesbian," "gay," "bisexual," and "transgender" are preferred. This is why the abbreviation LGBT has become a common appellation to capture all of these sexual identities. More recently, Q has been added to indicate both "Queer" and "Questioning," and some people include additional letters such as "I" (Intersex) and "A" (Asexual). Each of these terms is defined in the Glossary in Appendix A. It is thus not uncommon to see the acronym LGBTQIA+, with the plus-sign indicating that there are even more variations of sexual identity across a whole spectrum of possibilities.

For traditionalists, the term "homosexual" suggests that being lesbian or gay is an inalterable identity, an unchanging nature that is essential to one's being. While many traditionalists may acknowledge a genetic component to homosexual desires, they typically emphasize that acting on these desires is a voluntary choice. Thus, traditionalists are more likely to employ terms such as "same-sex attraction" and "same-sex preference" to underscore their position that same-sex relations are a matter of volitional behavior rather than inherent or essential identity.

In pursuit of fair and accurate portrayals of the various positions, this book will typically use the preferred terminology of the group under consideration at any given moment. Thus, traditionalist terms will be used when presenting the positions of traditionalists, and likewise for progressives. During times when both sides are being addressed together, "homosexuality" will be used as the default term. Two reasons warrant this approach. First, despite the objections from both sides of the cultural divide, "homosexual" is the most neutral term available in this highly volatile debate. Second, this is the term currently utilized in the *Book of Discipline,* the official account of church law and doctrine for the United Methodist Church.

17

CONCLUSION: EXPLORING OUR DIVISIONS

In the coming chapters, we explore the church's cultural conflict over homosexuality, and we consider the implications for the future of the United Methodist Church. At the heart of this exploration is this question: Given our shared love of God and neighbor, our mutual commitment to follow and serve Jesus Christ, and our common theological commitments to Scripture, tradition, reason, and experience, how is it that we as United Methodists can arrive at such markedly divergent opinions regarding the propriety of homosexuality in the life of the church? In other words, if we are united in these many ways, why are we so divided when it comes to homosexuality?

As we read the following chapters that highlight the divergent views of homosexuality in the United Methodist Church, let us approach these disputes in the spirit of Bishop Palmer's quote that opened this chapter. Let us thoughtfully consider the varying views within our denomination. Let us not talk past one another. Let us reason together. Let us strive to have a real conversation in which we truly endeavor to understand one another.

QUESTIONS TO CONSIDER

Consider the following questions. If you are discussing in a group, commit to a respectful dialogue in which the goal is hearing and understanding one another rather than winning and advancing a particular point of view.

1. Do you identify strongly with either the traditional or progressive view toward homosexuality? If so, how did you develop these beliefs? How many people do you know who think differently than you? How often do you discuss the issue of homosexuality with people of diverse views, and how civil are the discussions?

2. How optimistic or pessimistic are you that the United Methodist Church can resolve its internal divisions amicably? What accounts for this opinion?

3. Review the official positions that the United Methodist Church takes toward homosexuality. Which of these do you most strongly agree with? Do you disagree with any? If so, how do you disagree?

4. In your lifetime, what changes have you witnessed in people's attitudes about homosexuality? Where have the changes been the most pronounced in your experience? At work? At church? In your family? Have your own attitudes changed at all on this topic? If so, how?

5. Are you familiar with the Wesleyan Quadrilateral? Based on the brief overview in this chapter, which of the four do you think should play the most significant role as United Methodists deliberate the issue of homosexuality? Which do you think should be emphasized less? Why?

6. Which terms do you use when discussing homosexuality? Which ones are unfamiliar, confusing, or problematic for you?

Chapter 2

SCRIPTURE:
DIVIDED OVER THE BIBLE

THE POWER OF SCRIPTURE

Like many young people, I had many questions and doubts about my faith during my formative years. In my case, I was becoming disillusioned by the Church, especially the public face of Christianity that I saw in the media. I didn't understand how the Rev. Jerry Falwell (a fundamentalist televangelist) and the Rev. Jesse Jackson (a liberal civil rights activist) could both be men of the cloth who claimed to serve the same Lord and Savior, yet hold such diametrically opposing views on so many issues. Furthermore, I remember feeling like the Church was full of judgmental hypocrites, and I was fond of saying that many of my non-Christian friends acted more Christlike than my Christian friends.

When I went off to college, I met a young woman named Ingrid with whom I quickly became smitten. As we shared our hopes and dreams with one another, she told me about her strong Christian faith, and I revealed to her my frustrations with Christianity. I expressed my distrust of institutionalized religion, my disdain for religious hypocrites, and my skepticism toward dogmatic doctrines. I often repeated a litany of grievances to justify my apprehension toward fully embracing the Christian faith in which I had been raised.

Ingrid didn't try to rebuff each of my grievances with rational arguments or emotional pleas. Instead, her response to me was simple and straightforward: "Dale, you just need to focus on Jesus. That's all that really matters."

So that's what I did. I focused on Jesus, reading the gospels to see what the Bible said about the man from Galilee. I absorbed the stories about Jesus's birth, his life, his teachings, his miracles, his death, and his resurrection. I can't point to a particular moment when a lightbulb appeared over my head or when my heart was strangely warmed. But in the process of reading the Bible and learning about Jesus, my skepticism gave way to conviction, and my Christian faith took root in ways that continue to grow even today, more than 35 years later.

This is the power of Scripture.

(Side note: I ultimately had the good sense to marry Ingrid.)

UNITED METHODIST
UNDERSTANDING OF SCRIPTURE

United Methodist doctrine is clear: the Bible is the foundation for our discernment of religious truth. As the *Book of Discipline* states (¶105), "United Methodists share with other Christians the conviction that Scripture is the primary source and criterion for Christian doctrine." The *Discipline* describes the Bible as the "authentic testimony" of God's activity through all of human history. It testifies to what God has done, is doing, and will yet do. At the apex of the biblical witness is the life, teaching, death, and resurrection of Jesus Christ, the Word of God made flesh.

You are not likely to hear United Methodists, even theologically conservative ones, describe the Bible as "inerrant" or "infallible." It is more likely that you will hear adjectives like "authoritative," "trustworthy," and "reliable." The biblical authors, though limited and imperfect like all humans, were illumined by the Holy Spirit to create a testament of God's redemptive love that is both a "necessary" and "sufficient" witness of God's salvation through Christ. When people read the Bible, that same Holy Spirit can inspire and cultivate faith.

Though the Bible is the authoritative source of religious truth for United Methodists, fully understanding the biblical message requires an appreciation of context. The books of the Bible (39 in the Old Testament and 27 in the New Testament) were written over a span of approximately 1,500 years in a wide array of diverse cultures. Furthermore, the books of the Bible were written using many distinct literary genres: legal decrees, historical accounts, poetic songs, insightful wisdom, prophetic pronouncements, biographical accounts, instructional letters, and more. Understanding all of these various contexts is essential if one is to have a mature understanding of Christianity's sacred writings. Even then, specific portions of Scripture should never be read in isolation, for United Methodists believe that biblical passages should be interpreted "in light of their place in the Bible as a whole."

While Holy Scripture is definitively the primary source of our theological reflection for United Methodists, the *Book of Discipline* is also clear that our understanding of the Bible is reinforced by the other three segments of the Wesleyan Quadrilateral: Christian tradition, personal experience, and human reason. Some United Methodists have suggested that, rather than the concept of a four-sided quadrilateral, a more helpful image might be that of a three-legged stool. The Holy Bible sits on the stool, and this sacred Scripture is supported by the three legs of tradition, experience, and reason. If any of these legs is missing, our understanding of Scripture becomes unstable. Yet, in this analogy, there is no doubt that the Bible is the focal point of theological importance.

SPECIFIC PASSAGES ON HOMOSEXUALITY

For all the controversy surrounding the issue of homosexuality, the Bible does not place much direct focus on the subject. Only seven passages make specific reference to same-sex relations. Traditionalists believe these passages provide a clear, consistent biblical condemnation and prohibition against homosexual behavior. In contrast, progressives frequently call these passages "clobber verses," contending that they have been used to subjugate LGBTQ people at the expense of the broader, more inclusive message of Scripture. We will explore these seven passages in four groupings: the sin of Sodom (Genesis 19:4-11, Jude 7); the Holiness Code (Leviticus 18:22 and 20:13); Paul's lists of sins (1 Corinthians 6:9-11 and 1 Timothy 1:9-10); and Paul's description of unnatural relations (Romans 1:26-27). Not all of these passages carry equal importance in the United Methodist debate over homosexuality. For example, both traditionalists and progressives agree that the first chapter of Romans is pivotal. However, neither side of the cultural divide (at least within United Methodism) believes that the story of Lot's guests (Genesis 19) helps much to advance our biblical understanding of same-sex relations. Still, we will begin with a brief look at this latter passage and build toward the more relevant verses.[1]

The Sin of Sodom (Genesis 19:4-11, Jude 7)

The cities of Sodom and Gomorrah have become virtually synonymous with sin and depravity. Regarding sexuality, the city of Sodom became the root of "sodomy," and some Bible translations even use the word "Sodomite" to describe sexual immorality. This reputation stems from Genesis 19.

In Genesis 19, God sends two angels ("messengers") to Sodom and Gomorrah to confirm their great sin and injustice before destroying the wicked cities. Lot takes the strangers in to provide room and board for the evening. That evening, the men of Sodom surround Lot's home and shout (verse 5), "Where are the men who arrived tonight? Bring them out to us so that we may have sex with them." Lot pleads with the men to resist doing such an evil thing, and in verse 8 makes an alternative offer: "I've got two daughters who are virgins. Let me bring them out to you, and you may do to them whatever you wish. But don't do anything to these men because they are now under the protection of my roof." The mob refuses, and they do not back down until the messengers blind all the townsmen so they cannot find the entrance to Lot's home. Here is the passage:

> But before they retired for the night, all the men of Sodom, young and old, came from all over the city and surrounded the house. They shouted to Lot, "Where are the men who came to spend the night with you? Bring them out to us so we can have sex with them!"

---

1 Unless otherwise noted, the traditionalist and progressive positions described below draw upon widely held biblical interpretations within each theological faction. Thus, specific citations are kept to a minimum.

So Lot stepped outside to talk to them, shutting the door behind him. "Please, my brothers," he begged, "don't do such a wicked thing. Look, I have two virgin daughters. Let me bring them out to you, and you can do with them as you wish. But please, leave these men alone, for they are my guests and are under my protection."

"Stand back!" they shouted. "This fellow came to town as an outsider, and now he's acting like our judge! We'll treat you far worse than those other men!" And they lunged toward Lot to break down the door.

But the two angels reached out, pulled Lot into the house, and bolted the door. Then they blinded all the men, young and old, who were at the door of the house, so they gave up trying to get inside.

As we shall see in the next chapter, the Early Church presumed a strong theological connection between this story and homosexuality. However, contemporary United Methodists on both the right and the left generally downplay the passage's significance to the debate.[2] The actions of the angry mob were not those of consensual same-sex relations, but rather that of violent gang rape. Under no scenario would anyone attempt to justify the actions of these townsmen, so it does not advance our scriptural understanding of homosexuality. Nevertheless, some conservative scholars suggest that Sodom's sin is, indeed, related to homosexuality because of a New Testament reference to Sodom and Gomorrah. Jude 7 states, "Sodom and Gomorrah and the surrounding towns gave themselves up to sexual immorality and perversion." Most United Methodist scholars agree that this reference to sexual immorality is too broad and vague to justify a direct connection to homosexuality. It is not clear what actions the author of Jude was speaking of when he referred to the sexual immorality and perversion of these notorious cities.

Furthermore, when Sodom's sin is referenced elsewhere in the Bible, homosexuality is not the focus. Ezekiel 16:49 makes it clear that Sodom's

---

2 For an example of a traditionalist United Methodist downplaying the significance of this passage, see Richard B. Hays, "The Biblical Witness Concerning Homosexuality," in *Staying the Course*, eds. Maxie Dunnam and Newton Malony. This is a helpful article for many of the traditionalist positions discussed throughout this chapter.

-chief transgression was greed and inattention to those in need: "This is the sin of your sister Sodom: She and her daughters were proud, had plenty to eat, and enjoyed peace and prosperity; but she didn't help the poor and the needy." The next verse does condemn Sodom for doing "detestable things," but this phrase is used in the Old Testament Law for a host of transgressions, not solely same-sex relations. Similarly, when Jesus uses Sodom and Gomorrah as an example, it is not sexual deviance he is discussing, but their lack of hospitality. As Jesus sends out the twelve apostles, he instructs them to leave any city that does not welcome and listen to them, concluding, "it will be more bearable for Sodom and Gomorrah on the day of judgment than for that town" (Matthew 10:15). In particular, progressive Christians emphasize that these references in Ezekiel and Matthew indicate that the sin of Sodom was not homosexuality, but rather inhospitality, thereby nullifying any relevance to our understanding of the Bible's stance on same-sex relations.

The Holiness Code (Leviticus 18:22, 20:13)

The most direct condemnations of same-sex behavior in the Old Testament are found in the Book of Leviticus. There are two relevant verses:

> You must not have sexual intercourse with a man as you would with a woman; it is a detestable practice. (18:22)

> If a man has sexual intercourse with a man as he would with a woman, the two of them have done something detestable. They must be executed; their blood is on their own heads. (20:13)

Traditionalist View. For most traditionalists, these verses are explicit condemnations of same-sex behavior, at least same-sex behavior between men. In Leviticus 20:10-16, homosexual acts are included in a list that condemns other forms of sexuality that we still admonish today, namely adultery, incest, and bestiality. Traditionalists contend that if all these other sexual practices remain sinful in the eyes of the modern-day Christian, what basis do we have for making an exception for homosexual behavior? However, traditionalists are usually quick to emphasize that these passages make no reference to same-sex attraction or feelings; only the behavior is forbidden. Thus, individuals should not be denounced for having sexual yearnings toward people of the same sex, although acting on these feelings cannot be condoned.

Progressive View. Progressives believe that the two passages in Leviticus are culturally specific. There are many laws in Leviticus that Christians no longer follow because we assume that, rather than being mandates of God's timeless will, they were legal or ceremonial practices narrowly intended for the people of ancient Israel. Levitical decrees that Christians tend to ignore include the eating of shellfish (prohibited in 11:9-12), the blending of two different types of fabric together (prohibited in 19:19), and the tattooing of our bodies (prohibited in 19:28). Leviticus is full of similar restrictions that Christians no longer find binding or relevant, and progressive Christians include the laws against same-sex relations among the prohibitions that are now obsolete.

The debate between traditionalists and progressives over Leviticus 18:22 and 20:13 frequently rests on a disagreement over the type of law these verses represent. Many scholars divide the various decrees in Leviticus into three categories: (1) civil laws, the codes necessary to govern the Israelites; (2) ceremonial "purity" laws, the ritual requirements to remain clean and therefore holy before God; and (3) moral laws, the timeless ethical decrees that are binding for all people at all times. The challenging problem about these categories is that Leviticus does not explicitly make such distinctions, so there is not widespread agreement regarding the applicable category for each decree. Traditionalists contend that the same-sex prohibitions in Leviticus 18:22 and 20:13 are part of the moral law, God's eternal standard for all humans to follow throughout the ages. Thus, such behavior is "detestable" or an "abomination," as it is often translated. Progressives, however, believe that the ban on gay sex in Leviticus is more closely tied to the ceremonial purity laws that Christians do not adhere to, and therefore the condemnation of homosexuality is not an enduring moral decree. In this progressive view, the word "detestable" or "abomination" has more to do with ritual uncleanliness than with ethical wrongdoing.

Paul's Lists of Sins (1 Corinthians 6:9-11 and 1 Timothy 1:9-10)

It would probably be relatively easy for Christians to dismiss the two Levitical decrees prohibiting same-sex relations between men if the

New Testament was silent on the issue, but it is not. Three passages, all written by the Apostle Paul, address the topic. Consistent with the verses in the Old Testament, all three New Testament passages are critical of homosexual behavior. Below are two passages in which Paul lists immoral behavior:

> Don't you know that people who are unjust won't inherit God's kingdom? Don't be deceived. Those who are sexually immoral, those who worship false gods, adulterers, *both participants in same-sex intercourse*, thieves, the greedy, drunks, abusive people, and swindlers won't inherit God's kingdom. That is what some of you used to be! But you were washed clean, you were made holy to God, and you were made right with God in the name of the Lord Jesus Christ and in the Spirit of our God. (1 Corinthians 6:9-11, emphasis added)

> We understand this: the Law isn't established for a righteous person but for people who live without laws and without obeying any authority. They are the ungodly and the sinners. They are people who are not spiritual, and nothing is sacred to them. They kill their fathers and mothers, and murder others. They are people who are sexually unfaithful, and *people who have intercourse with the same sex*. They are kidnappers, liars, individuals who give false testimonies in court, and those who do anything else that is opposed to sound teaching. (1 Timothy 1:9-10, emphasis added)

These passages seem straightforward enough, but upon closer examination, understanding their relevance to the debate over homosexuality becomes more complex. To address this complexity, we will need to spend some time wading in the waters of biblical translation. When Paul lists homosexual acts in the passages above, he uses two Greek words: *arsenokoitai* and *malakoi*. These are rare terms, and it is necessary to explore their meaning. Not surprisingly, traditionalists and progressives have divergent understandings of how to interpret these unfamiliar terms.

Interpreting Arsenokoitai. *Arsenokoitai* is the rarer of the two words. It is not found anywhere else in the Bible other than the passages above. In fact, there is no evidence that anyone else in the ancient world used this term other than the Apostle Paul. Scholars typically assume that Paul coined the word precisely for use in his letters to Timothy and the Corinthians.

Traditionalists assert that Paul's meaning of *arsenokoitai* is closely linked to the Levitical prohibitions of same-sex relations that we examined in the previous section (Leviticus 18:22 and 20:13). The Septuagint is the earliest-known Greek translation of the Old Testament (the Old Testament was originally written in Hebrew). The Septuagint translates Leviticus 20:13 by incorporating the following two Greek words: *arsenos* (man) and *koiten* (bed). For most traditionalist scholars, it is clear that Paul has created the new word *arsenokoitai* by combining these two terms from the Greek translation of Leviticus. Thus, it is accurate to infer that Paul is rebuking all same-sex behavior (or, at a minimum, all same-sex behavior between men).

Progressive Christians are inclined to emphasize the vagueness of *arsenokoitai* and therefore contend that it is unwarranted to link it to homosexual practices, at least not so broadly. Many progressives believe that the indefinite terminology could be a narrower reference limited to exploitive same-sex practices. Examples of such sexual activity include the temple prostitution between men in Jerusalem, as well as the Roman practice of pederasty, sexual relations between an adult man with a boy. Both of these practices were not uncommon in the ancient world, and thus progressives contend that Paul may be denouncing only these particular same-sex behaviors.

Interpreting Malakoi. The Greek word *malakoi* is used in the passage from 1 Corinthians, but not in the letter to Timothy. The literal translation of *malakoi* is "soft." On the few occasions when the word is used elsewhere in the New Testament, it is used to describe soft clothing. So what does "soft" mean in this context? Scholars offer several possibilities. Most suggest that "soft" is a disparaging slang term for effeminate males. The euphemism may be alluding to soft, feminine complexion, or perhaps it is more directed at gentle, unmasculine behavior. Progressive Christians typically argue that it is not certain that Paul intends "soft" to be interpreted sexually. *Malakoi* may refer to one's demeanor, or it may suggest a character flaw such as weakness or cowardice. In either case, progressive scholars typically refute that *malakoi* has any clear and direct inference to sexuality. Indeed, the earliest English translations of the Bible, including the King James Version, translate *malakoi* simply as "effeminate."

Traditionalists suggest that there is a reason why Paul places *malakoi* alongside *arsenokoitai* in 1 Corinthians 6:9. By listing these words as a pair, Paul is denouncing the homosexual behavior of both partners in gay sex. He is writing against both the assertive "masculine" partner as well as the passive "effeminate" partner. Contemporary translations of the Bible often take this approach and link the two words together. The result is a condemnation of "men who have sex with men" (New International Version) or "both participants in same-sex intercourse" (Common English Bible).

Unnatural Relations and Creation (Romans 1:24-27)

We now arrive at the passage that many believe to be the most significant among the Bible's direct references to homosexuality. Paul's discussion of same-sex relations in the first chapter of Romans is noteworthy for several reasons. First, it is the only passage in the Bible that addresses homosexuality with more than a single sentence. Second, the verses in Romans go beyond a simple prohibition of same-sex behavior and frame the issue in a broader theological context. Finally, Romans 1:26 is the only verse in the Bible that explicitly addresses lesbian behavior. These are among the reasons that the verses in Romans are usually considered to be the pivotal passage to understand Scripture's stance on homosexuality, and for this reason we will give more attention to this passage.

The book of Romans is a profoundly theological book that addresses core Christian doctrines such as the depth of human sin and the need for God's grace through the atonement of Jesus Christ. The Apostle Paul lays the foundation for these ideas in the first chapter by asserting that all humans—Jews and Gentiles alike—have knowledge of God's "eternal power and divine nature." Although Gentiles are not aware of the Law that God directly revealed to the Jewish people, they nevertheless can see and understand the "invisible qualities" of God through the natural order of creation. Because God is revealed in creation (often described as God's "general revelation"), all humans are "without excuse" when it comes to sin; we can't plead ignorance (Romans 1:20).

Despite God's general revelation, Paul writes that people turned from God through their pointless reasoning, their darkened and foolish hearts, and their idolatry (1:21-23). Because humans rejected God, Paul writes that God "abandoned them," allowing people to act upon their morally corrupt desires. People chose to degrade their bodies, and they revered creation more than the Creator (1:24). Paul then provides an example of this type of debasing behavior that indulges one's sinful desires. That example is same-sex relations. Here are the key verses:

> 24 So God abandoned them to their hearts' desires, which led to the moral corruption of degrading their own bodies with each other. 25 They traded God's truth for a lie, and they worshipped and served the creation instead of the creator, who is blessed forever. Amen.

> 26 That's why God abandoned them to degrading lust. Their females traded natural sexual relations for unnatural sexual relations. 27 Also, in the same way, the males traded natural sexual relations with females, and burned with lust for each other. Males performed shameful actions with males, and they were paid back with the penalty they deserved for their mistake in their own bodies. (Romans 1:24-27)

Traditionalists and progressives agree that this passage uses same-sex relations to highlight humanity's sinful straying from God. Both factions also agree that Paul is not presenting an exceptionally new understanding of homosexuality, but instead, he is reflecting the prevailing assumptions of the culture of his day. This, however, is where the agreements end. Further interpretations of this passage diverge markedly, and we consider each view below.

Traditionalist View. For traditionalists, it is difficult to imagine how Paul could be any clearer. Same-sex relations are a form of trading God's truth for a lie and succumbing to the passions of creation rather than the will of the Creator (verse 25). Such behavior exchanges natural intimacy with the opposite sex for unnatural expressions with one's own sex. Paul's use of words like "creator" and "natural" are theologically crucial for the traditionalist. God created an inherent order in the universe, and within God's created order humans were endowed with an essential nature. An intrinsic part of that nature is the sexual union between a man and a woman.

For these reasons, traditionalists closely link Romans 1:24-27 with the creation accounts of Genesis. Genesis 1:27 reads that God creates humans—both male and female—in the divine image of God. God blesses them and gives the humans their first instructions, "Be fertile and multiply." Genesis 2 offers another account, with God declaring (2:18), "It's not good that the human is alone. I will make him a helper that is perfect for him." God forms a new human, a woman, from the rib of the original human, after which the original human declares that the woman is "bone from my bones and flesh from my flesh" (2:21-23). This decisive event concludes with Genesis proclaiming (2:24), "This is the reason that a man leaves his father and mother and embraces his wife, and they become one flesh."

Traditionalists interpret the above passages as a very intentional design to God's creation. God intentionally created humans both male and female to be complementary partners for one another. This is the natural order as God intended it from the very beginning. Thus, for the Apostle Paul, when individuals engage in gay or lesbian behavior, they are committing a willful distortion and rejection of God's intended order, and thus a rejection of God.

Progressive View. Progressives believe that to correctly understand Paul's theological denouncement of homosexual behavior in Romans 1, it is essential to thoroughly grasp the cultural context in which Paul was writing. Only when we consider the historical circumstances will we be able to understand what Paul means when he says that humans exchanged natural sexual relations for unnatural ones.

Progressives question what was meant by "unnatural sexual relations" in Paul's time. When ancient Jews spoke of intimate relations between members of the same sex, such relations during that era were commonly exploitive. One common form of homosexual activity was a type of prostitution performed as part of sacred rituals at pagan temples. Another practice among some Romans was pederasty, a sexual arrangement between an adult man and an adolescent boy. These were the typical homosexual practices known in Paul's day. Progressive and traditionalist Christians—whether in the past or the present—agree that such exploitive forms of sexuality are contrary to God's loving purposes for human intimacy. So where is the disagreement?

If Paul was writing about prostitution and pederasty, what would he make of today's same-sex relationships? Progressives believe that the Bible does not explicitly answer this question. Stated differently, progressives emphasize that people in Paul's historical and cultural context had no concept of loving, long-term, committed intimate relationships between two people of the same sex. The type of devoted relationships that LGBTQ Christians and their allies are endorsing were simply unknown.

In fact, progressives assert that there was no concept of homosexual orientation until the nineteenth century. Thus, all forms of same-sex intimacy would have been considered unnatural in the ancient world. As a modern consensus grows in support of the idea that a segment of humanity possesses an inherent homosexual orientation, progressives argue that it is crucial for Christians to alter their understanding of Paul's usage of "natural." For gay and lesbian people, their natural sexual preference is for people of the same sex. Thus, it would be unnatural for them to engage in heterosexual intimacy. For progressives, gay and lesbian people are fulfilling their natural, God-given desires when they commit themselves to loving, committed same-sex relationships. Such an understanding of "natural" would not have been feasible during biblical times, given the limited understanding of homosexual orientation during Paul's time.

JESUS AND HOMOSEXUALITY

For the Christian, the focal point of the Bible is Jesus Christ. When the United Methodist *Book of Discipline* gives its theological foundation for Scripture (¶105), it begins by prioritizing the significance of Jesus. The Bible is hailed as the source where "the living Christ meets us in the experience of redeeming grace" as well as the "authentic testimony to God's self-disclosure in the life, death, and resurrection of Jesus Christ." Furthermore, Jesus is called the "living Word of God" and the one who reconciles the world to God. Thus, Jesus Christ assumes a central place in the Christian's understanding and application of Scripture.

So what did Jesus say about homosexuality? Nothing. Absolutely nothing.

At least not directly.

Trying to infer someone's position based on their silence is a dubious endeavor, but that hasn't stopped many advocates on either side of the cultural divide from suggesting what Jesus's silence on homosexuality means. Some progressives argue that the topic of same-sex intimacy must not be a very central one if our Lord and Savior didn't address it specifically. If Jesus did not speak out against same-sex relations, why are so many of his contemporary followers investing substantial time and energy in reprimanding and restricting LGBTQ people? Traditionalists retort that there are countless issues that Jesus didn't overtly address but that we nevertheless consider crucial to Christian morality. Jesus is silent on other sexual topics like rape, incest, pedophilia, and bestiality. These behaviors were unquestionably immoral to Jesus's Jewish audiences, and thus needed no elaboration. Traditionalists contend that the same logic can be applied to the issue of homosexuality.

Arguments from silence are not especially helpful, but perhaps Jesus is not as silent regarding same-sex relations as he initially appears to be. Traditionalists and progressives agree that, rather than explicit proclamations, the teachings and actions of Jesus provide an implicit ethic about homosexuality. Not surprisingly, the two factions connect same-sex morality to very different aspects of Jesus's life and therefore come to very different conclusions about what Christians can infer from the life and teachings of Christ.

Traditionalist View. Traditionalist Christians contend that Jesus's teachings uphold the established Old Testament ethics for sexuality, including the prohibitions of same-sex relations as commanded in Leviticus. After all, Jesus declares in Matthew 5:17, "Don't even begin to think that I have come to do away with the Law and the Prophets. I haven't come to do away with them but to fulfill them." Furthermore, Jesus lists "sexual sins" as one of the behaviors that contaminate a person in the sight of God (Matthew 15:19; also Mark 7:21).

For the traditionalist, this preservation of traditional sexual morality is perhaps most evident when the Pharisees challenge Jesus about divorce in Matthew 19. Verse 3 begins the exchange: "In order to test him, they said, 'Does the Law allow a man to divorce his wife for just any reason?'" Jesus responds by quoting Scripture, namely the passages from Genesis (1:27; 2:24) that we have addressed earlier:

Jesus answered, "Haven't you read that at the beginning the creator made them male and female? And God said, 'Because of this a man should leave his father and mother and be joined together with his wife, and the two will be one flesh.' So they are no longer two but one flesh. Therefore, humans must not pull apart what God has put together." (Matthew 19:4-6; also Mark 10:5-9)

Jesus could have answered this question in any number of ways, yet he chose to directly quote a passage that speaks to the divine union of a man and a woman, whom God created male and female for this purpose. Traditionalists contend that Jesus is affirming the sacred and unique character of heterosexual marriage. Thus, while Jesus did not explicitly prohibit same-sex marriage in this passage, his Scripture-based description of marriage leaves no room for other forms of marriage in the minds of most traditionalists.

Progressives would largely agree with traditionalists regarding the value Jesus places on committed, covenant marriage. Progressives would disagree, however, that such a joining of two people into "one flesh" should be limited to unions between a man and a woman. The focus of Jesus's teaching, they would argue, is the sacred bonding and lifelong commitment between two people, and the biological sex of the individuals should be irrelevant.

Progressive View. When it comes to matters of sexuality, progressives often focus on the broad, foundational teachings of Christ. When Jesus is asked which commandment is the greatest, Jesus famously offers two: love your God with all your being, and love your neighbor as yourself. Jesus then concludes, "All the Law and the Prophets depend on these two commands" (Matthew 23:34-40). For the progressive, every other moral edict, including the same-sex prohibitions found in Leviticus, must be subservient to these two commands. Stated another way, our reading of Leviticus must be read through the lens of the Great Commandments, and that prompts the progressive Christian to emphasize an inclusive love that affirms LGBTQ individuals.

Furthermore, through both his teachings and his actions, Jesus has provided clear direction on how the love of one's neighbor should be enacted. When Jesus teaches about the sheep and the goats (Matthew

25:31-46), he proclaims that the sheep—those who will inherit the kingdom of God—are the ones who fed the hungry, offered drink to the thirsty, welcomed the stranger, clothed the naked, attended to the sick, and visited the prisoner. Jesus concludes this parable by identifying with each of these disparaged souls: "I assure you that when you have done it for one of the least of these brothers and sisters of mine, you have done it for me." For the progressive, LGBTQ individuals are systematically treated like "the least of these" in today's world. They have been marginalized, ostracized, and traumatized. Because LGBTQ people have been subjected to callous and homophobic prejudice and discrimination, followers of Jesus are commanded to reach out in radical love.

Jesus not only teaches radical love, but he also exemplifies it as well. Progressive Christians highlight the revolutionary way Jesus interacted with the outcasts of his culture: lepers, prostitutes, adulterers, the sick, the disabled, and more. Jesus's example of radical inclusion challenges his Church to go and do likewise, and progressives insist that LGBTQ people must be welcomed into the household of God in the same way Jesus welcomed those who were otherwise dismissed by the world.

Most traditionalists would agree with progressives regarding their focus on radical love toward LGBTQ people. Traditionalists would stop short, however, of translating that love of neighbor into an affirmation of their homosexual behavior. Whereas progressives believe affirming LGBTQ people and their sexual practices is a core part of loving them, traditionalists are more likely to emphasize that, while we are commanded to love the person, we are forbidden to condone the behavior. Traditional-minded Christians are apt to treat same-sex practices as the moral equivalent of adultery: Jesus shows compassionate love to the adulteress by saving her from stoning, and he doesn't condemn. However, he also tells her to go and sin no more (John 7:53-8:11).

BIBLICAL OBEDIENCE AND CHURCH LAW

With traditionalists and progressives varying so profoundly in their biblical interpretations regarding homosexuality, it's not surprising that the two camps also disagree sharply over their understanding of how best to "follow the Bible" on this matter.

Traditionalist View. United Methodist traditionalists place a strong emphasis on personal holiness when discussing homosexuality. The Wesleyan tradition believes that sexuality is a gift from God. However, like all God-given gifts, Christians have a responsibility to use these gifts lovingly in the way which God intended. For the traditionalist, Scripture provides a clear, straightforward mandate for how humans should act on their sexual desires, namely within the holy, God-ordained covenant of heterosexual marriage. Thus, for the traditionalist, biblical obedience means preserving personal holiness, and the Bible limits holy sexual behavior to the relations shared between a husband and wife within the sacred institution of marriage. Traditionalists believe that the present statements and statutes in the United Methodist *Book of Discipline* accurately reflect this biblical call to sexual holiness, concurring with the *Discipline* that the practice of homosexuality is incompatible with Christian teaching—and by extension inconsistent with Christian Scripture. Thus, regarding the issue of human sexuality, biblical obedience is tantamount to remaining faithful to the United Methodist *Book of Discipline*.

Progressive View. Progressives have a much different understanding of biblical obedience than traditionalists, but they resist the accusation made by some that they don't follow the Bible when it comes to the issue of homosexuality. In fact, after the 2012 General Conference, "biblical obedience" became a rallying cry for supporters of LGBTQ inclusion. Bishop Melvin Talbert made a landmark proclamation, encouraging all clergy to support LGBTQ people to defy the official church laws of the United Methodist Church by performing same-sex marriages. Rather than emphasizing personal holiness like the traditionalists, Bishop Talbert links biblical obedience to ideas of prophetic justice (Micah 6:8) and unconditional love (Mark 12:28-31). Jesus and the prophets call us to a higher love, one that breaks down barriers and welcomes the oppressed and the outcast. For progressives like Bishop Talbert, biblical obedience means a willingness to disobey unjust laws to remain loyal to the higher priority of God's love.[3] Thus, it is acceptable, even imperative, for Christians to disregard the unjust statutes in the *Book of Discipline* regarding homosexuality to express the loving, insistent, disruptive justice found in the Bible.

---

3 Melvin Talbert, "Disobey," in *Finding Our Way*, eds. Rueben Job and Neil Alexander.

Of course, traditionalists would clarify that they, too, care about justice and Christlike love. Similarly, progressives would argue that they also value personal morality and holiness. Nevertheless, the fact remains that, regarding the issue of homosexuality, the two blocs emphasize sharply contrasting visions of what it means to be biblically obedient.

CONCLUSION: DIVIDED OVER THE BIBLE

United Methodists share a love of Scripture and a firm conviction that the Bible should be the primary, authoritative source for understanding the love and the will of God. And yet, this chapter has summarized the deep division within the denomination regarding the best way to interpret and follow the Bible's direction regarding homosexuality.

For conservatives, the Bible is consistently clear: whenever same-sex relations are mentioned, such practices are uniformly, unambiguously rejected. The prohibitions are found in both Old and New Testaments, and the Apostle Paul provides theological reasoning for its condemnation. Jesus Christ recounts some of the earliest passages in Genesis that establish marriage as a holy institution between a man and a woman. If Scripture is truly going to be our primary source of discerning God's will, and if we are going to be holy in our personal behavior, Christians have little recourse but to proclaim homosexual practices as inconsistent with biblical principles of sexuality. We are still called to love our gay and lesbian brothers and sisters, and God's grace is available to all people. Furthermore, same-sex attractions and desires are not, by themselves, sinful. Nevertheless, we cannot condone acting on such desires to engage in homosexual behavior, as the Bible forbids it.

For the progressive, biblical references to same-sex practices don't encompass the totality of how same-sex relations are understood and expressed today. Same-sex activity as known in the ancient world— whether it be rape, pederasty, or temple worship—was exploitive, abusive, or sacrilegious, all worthy of condemnation. Progressives fight for LGBTQ inclusiveness because it reflects God's justice and God's love for those who are oppressed and marginalized. Mutually loving, sacrificial covenant love between two people of the same sex was unheard of in the ancient world, so the specific biblical passages don't speak to the type of loving, committed same-sex relations that progressives advocate. If Scripture is going to be our guide, progressives contend that we need to support same-sex couples in their desire to express covenant love as the Bible explicitly requires of us.

Traditionalists tend to be skeptical of the biblical interpretations of progressives. They believe that the biblical passages discussed in this chapter have a consistent and clear meaning that can be plainly understood with a straightforward reading of Scripture. Thus, conservatives view progressive interpretations as unnecessary and overreaching, an attempt to distort the simple truth of Scripture in an effort to defiantly make the Bible say something that it doesn't.

Progressives are equally skeptical about the biblical interpretations of traditionalists. They believe that traditionalists ignore the historical and cultural context of the "clobber verses" in the Bible—context that helps to make biblical meanings more transparent and more applicable to the realities of modern society. Thus, progressives view traditionalist interpretations as simplistic and outdated, an attempt to defiantly limit the openness and inclusiveness of God's grace.

There is little middle ground between these two stances toward a scriptural understanding of homosexuality, though some pastors and theologians have tried. For example, Adam Hamilton, pastor of a United Methodist mega-church as well as a best-selling author, has attempted to make a distinction between God's "ideal will" and God's "circumstantial will." God's ideal will for humans is heterosexual marriage, but there may be circumstances (such as a person's sexual orientation) in which God permits a "Plan B" (such as same-sex marriage).[4] This middle-ground approach to homosexuality has not garnered much support in the United Methodist Church. In fact, both sides of the debate typically find it objectionable. Traditionalists view it as a capitulation that ultimately results in legitimizing same-sex relations, while progressives maintain that such an approach relegates LGBTQ relationships to second-class status. Thus, the profound disagreements over a scriptural understanding of homosexuality continue to divide the United Methodist Church.

---

4 Adam Hamilton, *Confronting the Controversies*, Chapter 17, and *Seeing Gray in a World of Black and White*, Chapter 19.

QUESTIONS TO CONSIDER

Consider the following questions. If you are discussing in a group, commit to a respectful dialogue in which the goal is hearing and understanding one another rather than winning and advancing a particular point of view.

1. Review the summary of the United Methodist approach to Scripture near the beginning of the chapter. How consistent is the United Methodist position with your personal views of the Bible? Which positions and beliefs about the Bible are most important to you? How does this influence your approach to understanding moral issues concerning homosexuality?

2. Of all the specific Bible passages discussed in this chapter, which do you think are the most important to an understanding of homosexuality? Why do you find those to be the most crucial?

3. Reflecting on the specific Bible passages, are you more likely to agree with the traditionalist or progressive interpretations of each? Why do you find your preferred interpretation more convincing?

4. Are there any Bible passages that challenge you to reconsider your view of homosexuality? If so, which ones are they and why do you find them challenging?

5. Have you encountered other Bible verses that people use to address the issue of homosexuality? If so, what are these verses and how were they applied?

6. Envision Jesus discussing the issue of homosexuality with a gay or lesbian individual. What types of things do you picture Jesus saying? What Scripture would he be citing? Which of his words in the gospels would be applicable in such a conversation? What tone do you think he would be using?

7. What do you think of when you hear the phrase "biblical obedience"? Are you more likely to think of following a clear moral code of personal holiness or a commitment to pursue social justice? Even if you find both important, which would you prioritize, especially as it related to homosexuality? Why?

8. If someone wanted to discuss the Bible's view of homosexuality with you, how would you begin? What verses and key points would you emphasize? What tone or mood would you set for the conversation?

Chapter 3

TRADITION:
DIVIDED OVER THE CHURCH'S PAST

THE POWER OF TRADITION

I was born, baptized, and raised a Methodist. Both of my parents were born and raised Methodist as well. Throughout my formative years, my family attended a United Methodist Church, I worshiped in United Methodist sanctuaries, I attended United Methodist Sunday schools, and I was confirmed into the United Methodist Church.

All of this United Methodist pedigree, yet throughout my teenage years, I spent a good deal of time doubting my faith and seeking answers outside of my denomination. As a seeker, I spoke with people and read books from a wide variety of religious perspectives. During this time, I actively distanced myself from my religious roots and resisted labeling myself a United Methodist.

And still, during this time of wondering and wandering, my faith tradition had its grip on me. It's not a coincidence that the person with whom I fell in love and married—the person who shared such a similar moral and theological foundation with me that I wanted to spend the rest of my life with her—was also born and raised a United Methodist. It's not a coincidence that my wife and I ended up worshiping and serving as youth leaders at Methodist denominations. And after graduate school, when we began looking for a new church home and visited congregations from several other denominations, it's not a coincidence that the only congregations where we felt at home were United Methodist ones.

These events were not coincidences because, more than I am fully aware, my United Methodist upbringing has permeated my beliefs, my values, and my worldview. It has shaped the way that I read and interpret Scripture. It has molded my understanding of love, grace, holiness, and justice. It has formed my image of God.

Several years later, I was reminded yet again of the influence that my church tradition has had on me. After I experienced a profound calling to become a pastor (an experience that I discuss in the next chapter), I consulted the United Methodist *Book of Discipline* to learn more about the denomination's foundational values and ordination process. As I read over our official statement of theological beliefs, I was astonished to discover that the statements of United Methodist doctrine were a wonderful summary of my own beliefs. I had always assumed that I had formed my own unique religious beliefs during my years of spiritual wandering and seeking. Instead, it became undeniably clear that my core beliefs had been thoroughly shaped by my upbringing in the United Methodist Church.

That's the power of tradition.

UNITED METHODIST
UNDERSTANDING OF TRADITION

G.K. Chesterton, the clever and popular Christian apologist from a century ago, provides an insightful quip on the significance of tradition: "Tradition means giving votes to the most obscure of all classes, our ancestors. It is the democracy of the dead. Tradition refuses to submit to the small and arrogant oligarchy of those who merely happen to be walking about."[1]

The United Methodist Church shares Chesterton's reverence for the past. The *Book of Discipline* (¶105) opens its statement on Christian tradition by reminding us, "The theological task does not start anew in each age or each person." Rather than fashioning our faith from scratch, Christians are the beneficiaries of generations of faithful disciples of Jesus

---

1 G.K. Chesterton, *Orthodoxy*, 34.

Christ who have gone before us. The traditions that have solidified over time provide modern-day believers with a wellspring of wisdom that informs and strengthens our devotion to Jesus Christ during our particular moment in history. Tradition reminds us that we are not alone in our faith journey, and we do not need to reinvent the wheel. Instead, we can stand on the shoulders of the faithful Christians from ages past who inspire us and strengthen our resolve.

Tradition does not come to us as a single voice. Multiple Christian traditions have been passed down from different eras, different regions, and different cultures. Each has distinct lessons for our present generation, and we contemporary Christians must ascertain which features of the past are most applicable and edifying today in our pursuit to follow, serve, and honor Jesus Christ.

Of course, history is tainted by the human failings of the past, so our Christian tradition "includes a mixture of ignorance, misguided zeal, and sin." We must always be discerning about the heritage from which we draw, judging its merits by holding it to the eternal standard of Scripture. We strive to build upon the strengths of the past, growing in our collective capacity to love God and neighbor.

Each generation faces new and unique challenges in applying Biblical truths to their historical moment, and each era must strive to "interpret the truth of the gospel for their time." Nevertheless, much can be learned from the "cloud of witnesses" (Hebrews 12:1) that went before us, and we are imprudent when we ignore the wisdom of our forefathers and foremothers.

This chapter explores the ways that United Methodists understand and apply our tradition to the contemporary debate on homosexuality. We begin by taking a brief journey through the early centuries of Christian history, moving quickly to our Wesleyan heritage of the last two centuries. Much of the chapter is devoted to the past 50 years, from the time that the United Methodist Church became a new denomination.

HOMOSEXUALITY AND CHURCH HISTORY

Over the first 1,900 years of Church history, homosexual behavior has been decidedly condemned. This is a key reason why traditionalists today continue to oppose same-sex relations; they believe the beliefs of the past must be preserved to remain a faithful Church. This section provides a concise historical overview of the Church's views on homosexuality, beginning with the Early Church, continuing through the Middle Ages, and culminating with the Protestant reformers. Throughout these eras, three foundational beliefs emerge. First, the only natural form of sexual desire is that between a man and a woman. Second, God designed sexuality to be expressed within the context of marriage. And third, even within the confines of marriage, the purpose of sexual intimacy is procreation. The section concludes with an alternative approach to Church tradition—a prophetic tradition that emphasizes an expanding vision of God's justice for a broader range of people who have been marginalized throughout history, including LGBTQ people.

The Early Church

At the time when the Church was first emerging, the esteemed scholars Philo and Josephus wrote about homosexual behavior, associating it with the sin of Sodom in Genesis 19. These Jewish scholars likely influenced the early Christian Fathers. Clement of Alexandria (second century) and John Chrysostom (fourth century) both cited Sodom as an example of God's condemnation of homosexual practices. Chrysostom drew a parallel between homosexual behavior and Sodom: Just as same-sex intimacy is a "barren" practice because it cannot yield children, God's destruction of Sodom likewise made the land barren and infertile.[2] St. Augustine of Hippo (fourth century), often regarded as the most important among the Early Church Fathers, referred to the sin of Sodom as a sin against nature, a form of perverted lust that violates our relationship with God.

These references to Sodom notwithstanding, traditionalist United Methodist scholar Thomas Oden notes that, when assessing the morality of same-sex intimacy, the earliest Christian writers placed their main focus on the biblical passage from the first chapter of Romans. Though homosexuality was not treated as a uniquely terrible sin, Oden concludes that there was a complete and multifaceted consensus among the Early Church fathers regarding homosexuality: "It is grounded in idolatry, not simply lust as such. It dishonors the body. It tends divisively to pit male

---

2 John McNeill, *Church and the Homosexual*, 75.

against female. It does not yield the pleasure expected. It is a voluntary activity. It demeans human sexuality."[3]

Thus, the Early Church did not largely focus on homosexual acts, but when they did, the behavior was condemned. Church Father Tertullian sums up the attitude of the era well when he writes, "I should suppose the coupling of two males to be a very shameful thing." Such a denunciation was not limited to male homosexuality. An early Christian text called *The Apocalypse of Peter* chastises women "who lay with one another as a man with a woman," because they have defiled themselves.

The Middle Ages

The attitudes of the Early Church toward same-sex behavior carried over into the Middle Ages. As the Church amassed political power in Europe, Christian emperors issued decrees that banned men from marrying other men, or even pretending to act the role of a woman. By the sixth century, homosexual relations were punishable by burning at the stake. Eastern Roman Emperor Justinian outlawed same-sex behavior in fear that such acts would provoke God's wrath in Sodom-like destruction via earthquakes, famine, and pestilence.

Thomas Aquinas (thirteenth century) was perhaps the most influential theologian of the Middle Ages. One of his enduring contributions is a systematic elaboration of God's natural law, a set of eternal moral principles that can be deduced from rational inquiry. For Aquinas, homosexuality was an act against nature. Sexuality had a natural and intended purpose, namely procreation. Thus, any sexual act that did not create the possibility to propagate humankind was contrary to nature and therefore sinful. Such unnatural sexual activity would not be limited to homosexual behavior, but also acts like masturbation, oral sex, and intercourse using contraception. To Aquinas, to engage in sexual intimacy without the possibility of procreation was to use God's natural gift in a selfish and sinful manner.

Counter to the prevailing scholarship, progressive Yale historian John Boswell suggests that Christianity in medieval Europe actually displayed a level of tolerance, even acceptance. Boswell contends that the Christian

---

3 Thomas Oden, "The Classic Christian Exegesis on Romans 1:22-28," in *Staying the Course*, eds. Dunnam and Malony, 96.

ceremony of *adelphopoiesis*, which publicly unites two men or two women together, was the medieval equivalent of same-sex marriage.[4] Some progressives have pointed to Boswell's research as evidence that Christian tradition includes the affirmation of LGBTQ people. Critics argue that there is no evidence that *adelphopoiesis* ceremonies connoted a sexual relationship. Instead, traditionalist detractors assert that this sacred rite was more of a spiritual union between two people, like a platonic bonding of "blood brothers."

The Protestant Reformation

The early Protestant reformers of the sixteenth century brought new insights to God's saving grace through faith alone in Jesus Christ, but this novel theological outlook did not alter the enduring moral denunciation of homosexuality as unnatural. Martin Luther (sixteenth century), commenting on the story of Sodom in Genesis 19, focuses on the unnatural desires of the angry mob. He believes God has endowed men with a "passionate desire for the female." By demanding to have sexual relations with the male messengers, Luther declares that the sin of denying their natural passion and desire was of "unparalleled enormity." Luther further claims that such unnatural passion surely comes from the devil, who "extinguishes the fire of natural desire and stirs up another, which is contrary to nature."[5]

John Calvin assesses homosexual activity in his commentary on Paul's letter to the Romans. Calvin calls the same-sex acts in Romans 1:24-27 a "dreadful crime of unnatural lust." He also calls same-sex desires "beastly," and then proclaims that this sin is "beyond the beasts" because engaging in unnatural same-sex relations "reversed the whole order of nature." Calvin concludes by calling homosexual acts "disgraceful," "shameful," and "dishonoring of God."[6]

Given these attitudes towards same-sex relations, it's not surprising that homosexual practices were outlawed and severely punished in many countries during the time of the Reformation. In England, sodomy was

---

4 John Boswell, *Same-Sex Unions in Premodern Europe*.

5 Ewald Martin Plass, *What Luther Says*, 134.

6 John Calvin, *Calvin's Commentaries*, 79.

punishable by hanging. Similarly, in the New World, Puritan laws listed sodomy as a capital offense.

An Alternative Church Tradition

The brief summary above leaves little doubt that the Church has consistently disapproved of homosexual behavior throughout history. However, progressives often point to a different facet of Christian history that has shaped the Body of Christ. The Church has a long prophetic tradition in which inspired voices have answered God's call to challenge the harmful ways that God's people have misconstrued and distorted God's will. Prophetic voices call the Church to a higher love and a more just world.

The prophetic tradition traces its roots to the Old Testament prophets who are called by God to deliver a message of repentance and change when the people of God rebel and go their own way. Jesus Christ himself spoke prophetically when he repeatedly chastised the religious leaders of his day with proclamations like those in Matthew 23:23, "How terrible it will be for you legal experts and Pharisees! Hypocrites! You give to God a tenth of mint, dill, and cumin, but you forget about the more important matters of the Law: justice, peace, and faith."

For progressives, the prophetic tradition continually expands the love of God to a broader array of people. This vision of increasing inclusivity is seen in the earliest days of the Church. For example, in the Book of Acts, the Apostle Philip baptizes an Ethiopian eunuch (who were not allowed in temple courts), and the Council of Jerusalem proclaims that uncircumcised Gentiles have equal status among the disciples of Jesus (refuting arguments that they should first be circumcised). Both of these instances establish a church tradition in which the grace of God extends to a much wider range of people than previously imagined.

The *Book of Discipline* states (¶105) that the expansive, inclusive tradition of the Church continues to this day. Especially as we encounter Christian traditions from around the world, we "rediscover the biblical witness to God's special commitment to the poor, the disabled, the imprisoned, the oppressed, the outcast." Progressives emphasize the Church's historic role in serving as a visionary voice of love and compassion to those who have been marginalized in society. Over the past two centuries, the Church has been a voice of equality and justice in great social movements like the abolition of slavery, the suffrage movement, the civil rights movement, and the women's rights movement. Progressives see the fight for full equality of LGBTQ people—both in the Church and the broader society—as another faithful step in the prophetic tradition in the Body of Christ.

Of course, the Church has not always been true to its prophetic witness. The *Book of Discipline* reminds us that "the history of Christianity includes a mixture of ignorance, misguided zeal, and sin." Progressives are resolute that God is calling the Church to overcome the ignorance and misguided zeal it has displayed against LGBTQ people throughout history.

Progressives and traditionalists both agree that the prophetic tradition is an integral part of the Church's witness to God's expansive love and justice. The two factions diverge, however, in their understanding whether or not the prophetic reach of the Church should include the full inclusion of those who engage in same-sex relations.

For progressives, LGBTQ people have been excluded and marginalized by the Church in the same way as women and racial minorities. We are only a generation or two removed from Christians using widespread biblical justifications to segregate African Americans, and many Christian traditions still use scriptural reasons to keep women excluded from leadership and authority in the Church. Yet, faithful Christians have used their prophetic voice to welcome women and minorities into more complete (though still imperfect) inclusion in the Church and in the larger society. Progressives insist that the time is long overdue for the same type of inclusion and justice to be extended to followers of Christ who are LGBTQ.

For traditionalists, homosexual behavior is sharply distinguished from the historical experiences of women and racial minorities. Contemporary traditionalists in the United Methodist Church affirm that Scripture provides support for the inclusion of women and minorities. Scriptures like Galatians 3:28 proclaim that "there is neither slave nor free; nor is there male and female, for you are all one in Christ Jesus." Passages such as this provide biblical reasons for Christian tradition to fully include these historically marginalized groups into the life of the Church. However, traditionalists insist that the Bible is void of similar support for practicing homosexuals. In fact, they believe that the Bible consistently condemns such behavior, and thus it is wrong to equate the plight of women and racial minorities with the situation of LGBTQ individuals.

HOMOSEXUALITY AND WESLEYAN TRADITION

Two centuries ago, the ministry of John Wesley spurred a Christian movement that resulted the formation of a Wesleyan tradition, also called Methodism. Within this tradition are several separate denominations, of which the United Methodist Church is by far the largest. Wesley's influence remains vital to this day. Below is an overview of Wesleyan influences in the debate over homosexuality. The section begins with a summary of John Wesley's sparse comments on the subject, followed by a look at the divergent ways traditionalists and progressives draw upon Wesleyan tradition to justify their theological stance on LGBTQ issues. The section concludes with a brief overview of how our denomination has varying ways of applying John Wesley's classical call for a "catholic spirit" of unity among Christians.

John Wesley and Homosexuality

John Wesley said very little on the topic of homosexuality.[7] There is no mention of the issue in any of his voluminous sermons or journal entries. In his explanatory notes on the Bible, Wesley makes no reference to same-sex relations when commenting on the relevant Old Testament passages (Genesis 19:4-11; Leviticus 18:22, 20:13). Wesley is also silent when the Apostle Paul lists homosexual acts in 1 Corinthians 6:9-11 and 1 Timothy 1:9-10.

There are, however, two places where Wesley does address the topic. Commenting on Romans 1:26-27, Wesley refers to same-sex behavior as

---

7 Content from this section draws heavily from Kenneth Collins, "Human Sexuality and the Unity of the Church."

"unnatural lust,"[8] which is similar to the wording used in the King James Version of the Bible that Wesley would have used. Wesley attributes this behavior to "the heathen Romans" and then singles out the royalty, claiming "none more than the emperors themselves" indulge in such passions. Wesley also makes a brief note on Jude 7, where the King James Version states that Sodom and Gomorrah engaged in "fornication, and going after strange flesh." Wesley provides a short definition of fornication: "The word here means, unnatural lusts."

These sparse references suggest that the issue of homosexuality was not a primary concern for Wesley, but that he likely understood the matter within a larger context of natural law, inferring that heterosexual desire is an integral part of God's created order. Wesley takes a similar approach when he comments on Jesus's words on marriage in Mark 10. Wesley contends that the first humans were created distinctively male and female for the explicit purpose of being paired together: "God made Adam, when first created, male only; and Eve female only. And this man and woman he joined together, in a state of innocence, as husband and wife."

Given Wesley's relative silence on same-sex relations, United Methodists seek to frame the issue using other dimensions of Wesleyan tradition. As we shall see below, traditionalists tend to draw heavily from Wesley's insistence on moral purity, while progressives emphasize Wesley's widespread social concerns. For each of these positions, some introductory context will be necessary.

Traditionalist Emphasis on Personal Piety

Traditionalists often resist using terms like "LGBTQ" or even "homosexual." For them, such labels imply that sexual identity is a fixed and essential aspect of one's being, an enduring identity. A generation ago (and still today for many), traditionalists would have adamantly objected to such a characterization, insisting instead that homosexual behavior was a choice. For many traditionalists today, the source of homosexual desire is still an unresolved question, and thus they are hesitant to attribute it to a fixed identity or orientation. Traditionalists are therefore more likely

---

8 Wesley's biblical commentary is available at John Wesley, "John Wesley's Notes on the Bible."

to use terms like "same-sex attraction" and "sexual preference" because these phrases acknowledge the homosexual desire without conceding that such desire is inherent or inevitable.

The traditionalist focus on personal attraction, desire, and preference results in the belief that such passions can be resisted and controlled. This links same-sex desire to a host of other immoral and inappropriate behaviors upon which Christians call for self-control and abstinence. Alcoholics are not blamed for their yearning to drink, yet they are nevertheless held responsible for their choices and their actions. Similarly, traditionalists do not condemn individuals for their same-sex attractions, but they do maintain that acting on such desires breaches the will of God.

By defining homosexuality as an immoral behavior that can and should be resisted, traditionalists locate same-sex attraction in the Wesleyan tradition of piety and personal holiness. With both his words and deeds, Wesley emphasized the importance of individual moral behavior. As a young man, he led a "Holy Club" at Oxford University in which the members devoted themselves to, among other things, Bible study, prayer, fasting, healthy living, and personal accountability. This emphasis on moral living could also be seen in Wesley's theological concepts of Christian perfection and entire sanctification, by which Wesley meant that God's grace could so thoroughly transform individuals that their hearts' desire could be solely devoted to pleasing and glorifying God. Resisting same-sex attraction is just one unnatural and unholy passion among many that we must resist if we genuinely want to be released from our bondage to sin and restored back into the full image of God.

Progressive Emphasis on Social Justice

Progressives insist that the sexuality of LGBTQ people is far more than a simple matter of attraction or preference. Instead, it is an orientation, an identity, an inherent part of who they are. The homosexual desire for intimacy with people of the same sex is no more a choice than a person's heterosexual yearning for those of the opposite sex. For this reason, progressives are more likely to use terminology that defines sexuality as essential to one's identity. However, progressives also note that LGBTQ people should not be solely and narrowly defined by their sexual orientation, just as heterosexuals aren't.

With an understanding that sexual orientation is an inherent status, progressives more readily view LGBTQ issues as ones that affect the group. Rather than focusing on individual behavior, the emphasis is placed on how this community is being treated by others. Progressives identify people who are LGBTQ in the same way that people from other groups have been victims of social injustice—groups like the economically deprived, African Americans, and women. Adherents of the Wesleyan tradition have sought to alleviate the hardship and oppression of these groups throughout American history, and progressives believe similar efforts should be made on behalf of LGBTQ people.

In addition to his emphasis on personal piety, John Wesley was a social reformer. He opposed slavery. He preached in the open fields to thousands of struggling industrial workers. Wesley created a host of ministries to meet the social needs of poor people: schools, literacy programs, medical clinics, and shelters for the destitute. Later, Methodists adopted the 1908 Social Creed that specified a long litany of workers' rights. The first Women's Rights Convention was held in a Methodist chapel in Seneca Falls, New York. And Wesleyan churches were among the first to ordain women. For progressives, striving to ensure that LGBTQ people receive justice, equality, and inclusion—both in the life of the Church and in the broader society—is an extension of the social justice ministries that have distinguished the Wesleyan tradition from the very beginning.

Differences Over "Catholic Spirit"

Another feature of Wesleyan tradition that figures prominently in the debate over homosexuality is John Wesley's views on Christian unity amidst diversity. Wesley has a reputation for being broadminded, drawing wisdom and insight from a variety of Christian traditions and emphasizing areas of agreement much more than points of contention. Progressives and traditionalists differ, however, in the extent to which Wesley's inclusive impulse should be applied to the matter of homosexuality.

Progressive (and Centrist) View. Progressives and centrists often cite John Wesley's charitable attitude toward Christians who disagreed over non-essential issues. Bishop Ken Carter, who is currently the president of the Council of Bishops, provided an overview of Wesley's approach in a

2013 statement seeking a "generous orthodoxy" toward LGBTQ people.[9] He quotes John Wesley's familiar attitudes of openness toward differences of opinion: "As to all opinions that do not strike at the root of Christianity, we think and let think." Furthermore, Wesley downplayed the importance of rigid dogmas when he wrote, "Orthodoxy, or right opinions, is at best a slender part of religion, if it can be allowed to be any part at all."

Wesley's most famous statement of unity amidst diversity is his sermon "On a Catholic Spirit." Wesley elaborates upon the question asked in 2 Kings 10:15: "Is your heart right with my heart? If it is, then give me your hand." Bishop Carter quotes Wesley's elaboration of that passage, encouraging a similar spirit among United Methodists concerning our differences over homosexuality:

> "Is your heart right with my heart? If it is, give me your hand." I do not mean, "Be of my opinion." You need not. I do not expect or desire it. Neither do I mean, "I will be of your opinion." I cannot; it does not depend on my choice. I can no more think than I can see or hear as I will. Keep you your opinion; I mine, and that as steady as ever. You need not endeavour to come over to me or bring me over to you. I do not desire to dispute those points or to hear or speak one word concerning them. Let all opinions alone on one side and the other: only, "give me your hand."

As we shall see later in the discussion of United Methodist tradition, two moderately progressive pastors proposed that the *Book of Discipline* use "catholic spirit" language to frame the denomination's disagreement over homosexuality. Their proposal became a focal point of the 2012 General Conference, but it was ultimately voted down.

Traditionalist View. Traditionalists affirm John Wesley's view that all Christians exhibit a catholic spirit, but they also assert that progressives and centrists have misapplied the concept to the debate over homosexuality. Scholar and pastor Bill Arnold notes that Wesley's sermon on this topic was focused on different styles of worship, not matters of doctrine. Furthermore, Wesley's "Catholic Spirit" sermon later

---

9 Ken Carter, "'God Hath Bid All Humankind': Generous Orthodoxy and our Mission with Gays and Lesbians in the United Methodist Church." John Wesley's quotes in this section are included in Carter's reflection.

criticizes "latitudinarianism," a popular view in Wesley's day that warned of following strict doctrines too closely, for doing so was unhelpful and perhaps even harmful to Christianity. In contrast to latitudinarianism, Wesley insisted on holding firm to the "main branches of Christian doctrine," and he further encouraged Christians to avoid any "muddy understanding" of the faith.

Implying that the overly-tolerant approach of latitudinarianism resembles the moral laxity of United Methodist progressives, Arnold believes that the last half of Wesley's "Catholic Spirit" sermon is equally as instructive as the more celebrated earlier portion. He states, "Here we have a warning against the vagaries of broadmindedness, or uncritical tolerance, or any sort of indifference about exploratory theology." He concludes, "Wesley is certainly not advocating a laissez-faire or tolerant approach to Christian doctrine, as though unity in belief and doctrine is irrelevant as long as we have unity in mission and social justice."[10]

At the heart of progressive and traditionalist disagreement over Wesley's catholic spirit, then, is a question of where the boundary lies between non-essential opinion and indispensable doctrine. How broadly is the difference of opinion allowed to stretch among Christians? How far do we reach out to grab the other's hand? Some in the United Methodist Church are convinced that the breadth of our reach can encompass our differences over LGBTQ issues. However, there are others—those on both ends of the traditionalist-progressive continuum—who believe that the church's position on homosexuality is too central to the Christian faith to allow for substantial differences of opinion and action.

The above portrayals of traditionalist and progressive visions of the Wesleyan tradition should be read as general tendencies. The dichotomy is not so discrete in real life. Many traditionalists are concerned about issues of social justice, just as many progressives commit themselves to lives of personal holiness. In fact, one of the signature characteristics of the Wesleyan tradition is that personal piety and social justice are both a "means of grace" in which God works in us and through us. Nevertheless, it is accurate to say that each side of the cultural divide draws disproportionately from these two legacies of the Wesleyan

---

10 Bill Arnold, *Seeing Black and White in a Gray World*, 124.

tradition, and these two visions are increasingly portrayed as competing rather than complementary features of our faith. In the following section, we review in detail how homosexuality has become a perennially divisive issue throughout the last half-century when Wesleyan tradition formalized to become the United Methodist Church.

HOMOSEXUALITY AND UNITED METHODIST TRADITION

The United Methodist Church was formed in 1968 with the merger of the Methodist Church and the Evangelical United Brethren Church. Almost immediately, homosexuality became a perennial topic of discussion, debate, and division. This section explores the many features of United Methodist tradition and organization that is shaping the current crisis over LGBTQ matters in the denomination. The facets are numerous, and we shall explore several of them: the incompatibility clause, marriages and weddings, ordination of clergy, funding LGBTQ causes, denominational studies, special interest groups, protests, talk of schism, and shifting demographics.

This section will focus on the policies and deliberations of the denomination's General Conferences.[11] As a quadrennial international gathering with as many as 1,000 delegates, General Conference is the top legislative body of the United Methodist Church and the only entity that can set policy and officially speak for the denomination. Though the focus will be on the actions of General Conference, it will occasionally be necessary to include legal decisions by the Judicial Council (the "Supreme Court" of the denomination), as well as landmark events that occur in more regional contexts.

As we surmise the previous 50 years of United Methodist tradition regarding homosexuality, two consistent themes emerge. First, the denomination has affirmed the sacred value of LGBTQ people and

---

11 The details in this section come from numerous articles and documents. In addition to official United Methodist sources, Tiffany Steinwert's Ph.D. dissertation, "Homosexuality and the United Methodist Church: An Ecclesiological Dilemma," provides an exceptionally thorough account of the denomination's deliberations over homosexuality from 1968-2008.

is committed to the protection of their civil rights. Second, General Conferences have drawn decisive limits on the affirmation and participation of LGBTQ people in the life of the church. In contrast to the increasing acceptance of homosexuality in the United States, over the past half-century the United Methodist General Conference has consistently maintained, and in some cases even increased, the restrictions placed on LGBTQ people within the denomination.

The Incompatibility Clause

At the inaugural United Methodist General Conference in 1968, delegates approved a Commission on Social Principles to develop a unified social creed for the new denomination. Four years later at the 1972 General Conference, the commission presented a declaration of social principles that included a statement on homosexuality. The initial proposal affirmed the sacred worth of homosexuals and made no moral condemnation of same-sex behavior:

> Homosexuals no less than heterosexuals are persons of sacred worth, who need the ministry and guidance of the Church in their struggles for human fulfillment, as well as the spiritual and emotional care of a fellowship with God, with others, and with self. Further we insist that all persons are entitled to have their human and civil rights ensured.

When the debate reached the floor of the 1972 General Conference, much controversy ensued. The commission had intended the statement to be morally neutral, but many delegates believed it read more like an affirmation of same-sex behavior. As deliberation drew to a close, a delegate moved to add the following clause at the end of the statement:

> ...though we do not condone the practice of homosexuality and consider this practice incompatible with Christian teaching.

This stipulation, now known as the "incompatibility clause," was amended to the initial statement, and the amended declaration passed with a majority vote. The United Methodist Church was formally on the record as opposing homosexual behavior.

At every General Conference since then, delegates have considered petitions to remove or reword the incompatibility clause. Each time, the motions have been defeated, typically with over 60% of the delegates voting to retain the phrase in its original form. Thus, the incompatibility clause has been part of United Methodist tradition throughout its history.

Over the years, General Conference has incorporated some affirming context to clarify that, while same-sex behavior is inappropriate, the denomination nevertheless supports LGBTQ people. In 1988, delegates added details immediately following the incompatibility clause: "Although we do not condone the practice of homosexuality and consider this practice incompatible with Christian teaching, we affirm that God's grace is available to all. We commit ourselves to be in ministry for and with all persons." In 2000, yet another sentence of support was added, stating, "We implore families and churches not to reject or condemn their lesbian and gay members and friends."

After repeated failed attempts to overturn the incompatibility clause, some centrist and progressive delegates began advocating for language that acknowledged the denomination's lack of agreement over homosexuality. These efforts, too, have been consistently rebuffed. In 1996, a resolution that United Methodists were "unable to arrive at a common mind" was soundly defeated. In 2000, delegates voted down a proposal to change the incompatibility clause from "although we do not condone the practice of homosexuality..." to "although *many* do not condone...." In 2004, delegates approved a minimal revision. The wording of the incompatibility clause was changed from *"we* do not condone..." to *"The United Methodist Church* does not condone...." (emphasis added).

A final push to formally recognize the denomination's division over homosexuality came in 2012 when two prominent and centrist pastors, Adam Hamilton and Mike Slaughter, drew upon Methodist tradition and used the words of John Wesley in their proposed revision to the *Book of Discipline*. Their proposal would have removed the incompatibility clause and replaced it with:

> We commit to disagree and respect with love, we commit to love all persons and, above all, we pledge to seek God's will. With regard to homosexuality, as with so many other issues, United Methodists adopt the attitude of John Wesley who once said,

"Though we cannot think alike, may we not love alike? May we not be of one heart, though we are not of one opinion? Without all doubt, we may."

Like all previous proposals to revise the incompatibility clause, 55% of the delegates voted to decline the new wording, opting to retain the original language. Thus, for over four decades the official position of the United Methodist Church has remained: "The United Methodist Church does not condone the practice of homosexuality and considers this practice incompatible with Christian teaching."

Marriages and Weddings

In addition to the incompatibility clause, the 1972 General Conference adopted a statement in the Social Principles that declares, "We do not *recommend* marriage between two persons of the same sex." At the next General Conference four years later, that language was toughened to read, "We do not *recognize* a relationship between two persons of the same-sex as constituting marriage" (emphasis added in both statements). Today, the *Book of Discipline* continues to authorize only heterosexual marriage, stating, "We support laws in civil society that define marriage as the union of one man and one woman." Furthermore, in 1996, General Conference voted to prohibit United Methodist clergy and churches from involvement with same-sex union ceremonies. The statement pronounced, "Ceremonies that celebrate homosexual unions shall not be conducted by our ministers and shall not be conducted in our churches."

The 1996 prohibition on same-sex marriage was soon put to the test. In 1997, controversy erupted when United Methodist minister Jimmy Creech officiated the union ceremony of two women. Creech was brought up on church charges for violating church law. The Judicial Council initially acquitted Creech of the charges, reasoning that the restrictive statements about same-sex marriage were found in the Social Principles section of the Discipline, and therefore were merely instructive guidelines that did not carry the full weight of church law. However, Creech was eventually defrocked as a United Methodist minister when he was charged again after presiding over another same-sex marriage ceremony, this time for two men. In this second case, the Judicial Council ruled that the Social

Principles do, indeed, have the effect of church law. Chapter 4 provides details of these events.

In 2004, shortly after Massachusetts became the first state to legalize same-sex weddings, General Conference declared that "conducting ceremonies that celebrate homosexual unions and performing same-sex wedding ceremonies" were chargeable offenses for which United Methodist clergy could be brought to a church trial. General Conference added further restrictive language to the Social Principles in 2008, declaring that "although all persons are sexual beings whether or not they are married, sexual relations are affirmed only within the covenant of monogamous, heterosexual marriage."

Ordination of Clergy

The United Methodist Church was still in its infancy when issues of sexual orientation and the ordination of clergy first arose. In 1971, after openly acknowledging that he was gay, clergyman Gene Leggett of the Southwest Texas Conference was charged by his annual conference as unacceptable for ministry. By a vote of 144-117, his clergy credentials were revoked. This incident prompted the defrocked Leggett to attend the 1972 General Conference as a lobbyist on behalf of gay and lesbian people, and his dialogue with the legislative committee shaped the initial statement on homosexuality prior to the addition of the incompatibility statement (see above). Leggett was also one of the founders of the United Methodist Gay Caucus in 1975. This organization eventually became known as Affirmation, which still advocates on behalf of LGBTQ United Methodists today.

Leggett's dismissal was a local action by his annual conference. Throughout the first decade of the United Methodist Church's formation, there remained an ambiguity regarding the ordination of LGBTQ individuals. The *Book of Discipline* firmly declared that homosexuality was incompatible with Christian teaching, but there were no formal restrictions concerning same-sex relations for United Methodist clergy. The 1980 General Conference attempted to address this inconsistency, but delegates narrowly rejected a petition that would have formally forbidden any "self-avowed practicing homosexual" from being ordained. At the same time, delegates upheld the incompatibility clause, so the ambiguity remained.

In the midst of this ambiguity, in 1982 the Rocky Mountain Annual Conference ordained an openly lesbian woman, and the Judicial Council ruled that the United Methodist ordination standards did not explicitly include restrictions on the ordination of an openly gay candidate. While acknowledging the complex and sensitive nature of the issue, the Judicial Council declared, "Our authority ... is to interpret the existing law of the church and we find no provision making same-sex orientation a disqualification for ordination."[12]

Addressing this issue, the 1984 General Conference added language to the ordination guidelines that definitively excluded LGBTQ people. "Fidelity in marriage and celibacy in singleness" became the standard for all ordained clergy, and the delegates added an additional prohibition to the *Discipline*: "Since the practice of homosexuality is incompatible with Christian teaching, self-avowed practicing homosexuals are not to be accepted as candidates, ordained as ministers, or appointed to serve in the United Methodist Church."[13] For more than three decades, this has been an official standard of ordination for the denomination. This policy was further toughened in 2004 when, in an exceptionally narrow 455-445 vote, delegates decreed that being "a self-avowed practicing homosexual" was now a chargeable offense for United Methodist clergy, potentially subjecting them to a church trial. The following day, progressives staged one of the largest protests ever at a General Conference.

Funding LGBTQ Causes

For more than four decades, General Conference has restricted funding for advocacy of LGBTQ causes. In 1976, delegates voted to prohibit funding in three ways. First, they ordered the Council on Finance and Administration to "ensure that no board, agency, committee, commission, or council shall give United Methodist funds to any 'gay' caucus or group, or otherwise use such funds to promote the acceptance of homosexuality." Second, they directed United Methodist boards and agencies to use funds

---

12 Judicial Council Decision 513, 1982.

13 The *Book of Discipline* (¶304.3) states that "'Self-avowed practicing homosexual' is understood to mean that a person openly acknowledges to a bishop, district superintendent, district committee of ordained ministry, board of ordained ministry, or clergy session that the person is a practicing homosexual."

"only in support of programs consistent with the Social Principles of the Church." Third, they prohibited "funds for projects favoring homosexual practices."[14] These three funding restrictions have remained intact since that time, with some relatively recent revisions. In 2004, General Council expanded the funding restrictions to apply not only to General Conference and its agencies but also to all annual conferences.[15]

In 2012, General Conference incorporated language that attempted to balance the restrictions, declaring that United Methodist funds could not be used for either the promotion or opposition of LGBTQ causes. The restriction states that no annual conference agency can use funds "to promote the acceptance of homosexuality or violate the expressed commitment of The UMC 'not to reject or condemn lesbian and gay members and friends' (¶161F)."

Progressive Reaction: Protests

From the earliest years of United Methodism, petitions and protests have been an integral part of General Conference. At the special session called in 1970, a 40-foot banner was unfurled that proclaimed, "Bullshit," though no one seems to recall the motives behind the expletive. By the 1990s, progressive protests for LGBTQ inclusion and justice became a regular feature at most every General Conference. The demonstrations typically involved protesters parading through the convention hall carrying banners with declarations like "The Stones Will Cry Out" and singing lyrics such as "I am the church! You are the church! We are the church together!" At times, protesters have interrupted the actual proceedings of General Conference with tactics like stomping on the bleachers to drown out delegates who were speaking.

The protests at the 2000 General Conference in Cleveland were especially disruptive. Progressive United Methodists, supported by the national organization Soulforce, staged a massive protest outside of the conference's convention center. Over 300 protesters took turns blocking the convention center doors, and nearly 200 people were arrested for

---

14 See Tiffany Steinwert, "Homosexuality and the United Methodist Church," 51.

15 The new stipulation also clarified that there were two exceptions to these restrictions. Funding was permitted for educational efforts concerning homosexuality, so long as they were fair-minded and consistent with United Methodist policies. Also, resources for HIV-related ministries would not be impeded by the new statute.

aggravated disorderly conduct. The following day, protests continued. This time the demonstrations were inside the convention center, and 30 protesters (including two bishops) were arrested on the conference floor, a historic first. Supporters yelled, "Shame!" as the police detained the protesters, also accompanied by choruses of "We Shall Overcome." In a dramatic moment, one distraught protester postured herself to fall from a balcony ledge before others clutched her back to safety.

Sometimes dissenters have disturbed sacred space during their protests. One of the more controversial moments of the 2004 General Conference occurred when one frustrated protester took a communion chalice off the altar and threw it to the ground, smashing it to pieces. In 2008, the communion table was again a target of protest, as demonstrators draped a black shroud over the altar as a sign of mourning.

Traditionalist Reaction: Talk of Schism

As early as 1976, some were calling homosexuality "potentially the most divisive" issue facing the denomination. Curiously, although it has been progressives who regularly protest the injustice of United Methodist policies, it is the traditionalists who are at the forefront of calls for separation and schism. Murmurings and vague suggestions of schism first arose in 2000,[16] but the topic took center stage at the 2004 General Conference in Pittsburgh. Giving a speech at a breakfast gathering for traditionalists, Bill Hinson, a megachurch pastor and president of the traditionalist Confessing Movement, made a public declaration that it was time to openly discuss a formal separation of the United Methodist Church:

> I believe the time has come when we must begin to explore an amicable and just separation that will free both sides from our cycle of pain and conflict. Such a just separation will protect the property rights of churches and the pension rights of clergy. It will also free us to reclaim our high calling and to fulfill our mission in the world. Therefore, let us, like Paul and Barnabas, agree to go our separate ways.[17]

---

16 See Steinwert, "Homosexuality and the United Methodist Church," 2, 46.
17 Bill Hinson, "Is It Time for an Amicable and Just Separation?"

The talk of schism became a significant cause for concern among many delegates, and before the end of the 2004 General Conference, delegates had passed a resolution of unity with 95% approval. The resolution declared, "As United Methodists we remain in covenant with one another, even in the midst of disagreement, and affirm our commitment to work together for our common mission of making disciples throughout the world."

Despite the show of unity, talk of schism soon became commonplace. The topic took center stage once again in 2014 when a formal proposal of separation surfaced in anticipation of the next General Conference. A group of 80 conservative pastors and theologians issued a statement that cited deep divisions over obedience to church law, the authority of Scripture, and interpretations of personal and social holiness. Known as "The Memphis Declaration," the statement reflected the same themes of cordial separation as Hinson's speech from a decade earlier. It stated, "In the manner that Paul and Barnabas chose to part amicably (Acts 15:39-41), can we not work for a way of parting that honors the sincerity of those with whom we differ and no longer brings pain to persons made in the image of God?" This call for amicable separation from traditionalist leaders has played a prominent role in the current crisis, a topic we revisit in greater detail in Chapter 6.

Shifting Demographics

The General Conference of the United Methodist Church is a legislative body comparable to the House of Representatives in the United States. Just as the number of House representatives from each state can shift every decade based on census population statistics, so too does the distribution of General Conference delegates change in each region based on changing membership numbers. The demographic shifts in the United Methodist Church have played a profound role in establishing an enduring conservative tradition on matters regarding homosexuality.

Two demographic trends are especially significant. The first trend is occurring within the United States. Membership in the United Methodist Church has become increasingly concentrated in the most conservative regions of the nation. The denomination divides the United States into five jurisdictional regions: Northeastern, Southeastern, North Central,

South Central, and Western (See the map in Appendix C). United Methodist membership has decreased in all five of these regions in recent years, but the drop has been less pronounced in the Southeastern and South Central jurisdictions. Together, these two jurisdictions comprise 60% of all United Methodist members in the United States. These are also regions where opposition to homosexuality is strongest. Thus, the United Methodist Church is becoming more concentrated in the conservative areas of the United States. These jurisdictions, therefore, have increasing representation at General Conference, which ultimately determines policy on LGBTQ issues for the denomination.

The second demographic trend is perhaps even more significant. The United Methodist Church is a global denomination. While much attention is given to the controversy over homosexuality within the United States, General Conference delegates also hail from Africa, Europe, and the Philippines. Of these regions, Africa is by far the fastest-growing region of the denomination. In fact, with membership decline in the United States and increase in Africa, the two areas are becoming increasingly similar in size. Currently, the United States has 6.9 million members, which is 55% of all members globally. African membership has grown to nearly five million, which is about 40% of United Methodism. All other regions combined comprise less than 5% of the denomination.

The growing number of African delegates at General Conference has had a profound impact on the homosexuality debate. Generally speaking, African traditions are steadfastly opposed to homosexual behavior, and African Christians as a whole don't believe that this is an issue that has room for negotiation or compromise. African delegates have made impassioned pleas at General Conference, warning that their congregations would perceive any concession on LGBTQ issues as a betrayal that might eventually kill the church in Africa.

The numbers tell a very clear story. Nearly a third of all General Conference delegates now come from African nations, and these delegates are almost unanimous in their opposition to homosexuality. Furthermore, a substantial majority of the representatives from the United States represent the two most conservative jurisdictions. Together, this traditionalist coalition of Africa and the southern U.S. now accounts for nearly two-thirds of all delegates who attend General Conference. Thus, United Methodist progressives see little hope of the denomination softening its stance toward same-sex relations.

CONCLUSION: DIFFERENT
STREAMS OF TRADITION

Like the deep divisions over the interpretation of Scripture, traditionalists and progressives are at odds over the meaning of their shared Christian tradition as it applies to the issue of homosexuality. Traditionalists see an unbroken legacy of faithful commitment to the biblical principle of covenant love between a man and a woman, who were each created by God and endowed with a natural bond of desire for one another. Conversely, progressives see a long history of exclusion for a wide range of marginalized groups, and thus they embrace a prophetic tradition that corrects the injustices of the past and advocates for the full inclusion of LGBTQ people. Both of these streams of tradition can be seen flowing from biblical times and the Early Church up through this present moment. Both sides of the cultural divide in the United Methodist Church justify their positions by drawing upon the legacy of John Wesley.

In the United States, attitudes toward homosexuality have become increasingly accepting, most clearly evident in the 2015 Supreme Court decision to legalize same-sex marriage. Adapting to these trends, many mainline Protestant denominations—including those from Lutheran, Presbyterian, and Episcopalian traditions—have softened their positions on homosexuality to allow for the ordination of LGBTQ clergy and for the celebration of same-sex marriages. This is not, however, the case for United Methodists. Over its 50-year history, the United Methodist Church has maintained, and in many ways toughened, its opposition to same-sex relations. The two most influential regions of United Methodism, African countries and the southern part of the United States, are both strongholds of traditional views toward homosexuality. This makes it very unlikely that the denomination will change its position any time soon, barring a radical departure from the status quo.

QUESTIONS TO CONSIDER

Consider the following questions. If you are discussing in a group, commit to a respectful dialogue in which the goal is hearing and understanding one another rather than winning and advancing a particular point of view.

1. When you think of Christian tradition, what immediately comes to mind? What aspects of tradition are most important to your faith journey? Do any of these facets of tradition inform your opinions about homosexuality?

2. Review the Church's approach to homosexuality during the times of the Early Church, the Middle Ages, and the Protestant Reformation. Do any ideas or theologians stand out as particularly important to you? How do you think these eras may have influenced our current understanding of homosexuality?

3. When you think of the prophetic tradition within the Church, what issues come to mind? Which groups have been treated more justly because of Christianity's prophetic tradition? How did the Church handle these issues well? How did they handle them poorly? How do these issues compare to the current debate over homosexuality?

4. When you think of John Wesley, what features of his ministry and legacy do you think have influenced you the most? Are these features more consistent with the traditionalist emphasis on personal piety or the progressive focus on social justice? How so? How do these two strands of Wesleyan tradition influence your own views of homosexuality?

5. Reflecting upon the United Methodist tradition regarding homosexuality, were there any moments or trends that you found surprising? Were there any policies that you didn't know about? How would you characterize the overall history of United Methodism's handling of issues regarding homosexuality?

6. What is your opinion of the "incompatibility clause," which states that the practice of homosexuality is incompatible with Christian teaching? If you were writing a statement that summarized your personal beliefs on homosexuality, what would it say?

7. Consider how the United Methodist Church has handled policies regarding the celebration of same-sex weddings, the ordination of LGBTQ clergy, and the funding of LGBTQ causes. Do you think the denomination has dealt with these issues well? If not, how would you change any of these policies?

8. What is your opinion of the progressive tactic of protesting at General Conferences? What is your view of the traditionalist call for an amicable separation? Do you see either of these approaches as constructive? Do you see either as damaging? How so?

9. Given the changing demographics in the United Methodist Church (growing influence in the most traditionalist regions), how do you think this will affect the denomination over the next several years? How will this influence the debate over homosexuality?

Chapter 4

EXPERIENCE: DIVIDED OVER THE SPIRIT'S WORK

THE POWER OF EXPERIENCE

Pastors often speak of their decision to become ministers as a "calling." When I speak of my own calling, I mean it quite literally.

I became a pastor at age 37. There was no pressing reason for me to pursue the ministry. I had a great job as a tenured professor at a beautiful college. One day, I was enjoying the stunning scenery of my campus with a bike ride in the woods. As my mind wandered, I began to contemplate a serious crisis at the school. Our college was struggling with our religious identity, debating the appropriate balance between our commitment to our Christian heritage and our desire to welcome people of all faiths. A series of controversial events had greatly upset friends and colleagues on both sides of the debate—those who hoped the college would more robustly embrace its Christian identity and those who desired a more pluralistic campus.

It would be wrong for me to say that I was praying about the religious tension on campus during my bike ride, but I was intensely pondering how I could be helpful in the matter. The divisiveness had become very unhealthy and disruptive, and I wanted to lend my support to ease the strain however possible.

Then I heard a voice. It wasn't a booming voice coming down from heaven. It wasn't even audible. Rather, the voice I heard was silent and internal. Nevertheless, the voice I heard was just as real to me as if I was having a face-to-face conversation.

The voice spoke a single word: "Prepare."

Prepare. I cannot tell you why, but I intuitively interpreted this to mean that I should prepare to serve as my college's chaplain one day. I began looking into the process of becoming a United Methodist minister. Stepping out in faith, I began the journey toward becoming a pastor.

I estimated that it would take me about six years to be prepared enough to fulfill God's calling to be my college's chaplain. Instead, through a series of improbable (or should I say providential?) events, six years transpired into only six weeks. During a completely unrelated meeting with my college president, I serendipitously learned that the current chaplain was planning to resign. I took the opportunity to tell the president about my recent plans to become a minister—though I must confess that I left out the part about God speaking to me in the woods. Soon after that conversation, the president asked me to serve as the college's acting chaplain. A year later, I was hired as the permanent chaplain.

In the ensuing years, I believe that God used my chaplaincy to help define my school's religious identity and to ease the tensions on campus. Through it all, I hope and trust that God was honored and glorified through my ministry.

That's the power of experience.

UNITED METHODIST UNDERSTANDING OF EXPERIENCE

John Wesley was not being especially innovative with three of the four theological tools that eventually became known as the Wesleyan Quadrilateral. Scripture, tradition, and reason were all standard resources for theological reflection in Wesley's Anglican upbringing. However, what was distinctive about Wesley's four-pronged approach was the fourth prong: experience. Perhaps it should not be surprising that the man who felt his "heart strangely warmed" by God would consider experience an important means of Christian understanding and insight.

Our personal experiences are singular and fleeting, but they can affirm the universal and eternal truths found in the Bible. The *Book of Discipline* states that United Methodists use experience to reveal "confirmations of the realities of God's grace attested in Scripture." It further states, "Our experience interacts with Scripture." Experiences shape how we read Scripture, but our reading of Scripture also shapes and defines our experiences. These Christian experiences not only provide us with the assurance of God's mercy in our lives, but they also give us new life in Christ and "new eyes to see the living truth in Scripture."

Possibly because it is an innovative addition to theological inquiry, experience is often misunderstood by United Methodists. Two things are particularly significant for a proper perspective on the theological dimensions of personal experience. First, it is important to note that experience should be both individual and corporate. It involves not only our inner feelings but also the collective experiences that we share with one another as we live and love in the world. As the *Book of Discipline* states, "Although profoundly personal, Christian experience is also corporate; our theological task is informed by the experience of the church and by the common experiences of all humanity. In our attempts to understand the biblical message, we recognize that God's gift of liberating love embraces the whole of creation."

Second, our personal experience properly informs our theological understanding only insofar as it is guided and illuminated by the Holy Spirit. Just as not all tradition is good, and just as all reason does not lead to truth, so too with experience: not all of our experiences are inspirations from God. The authenticity of our experiences must be checked by our other theological guidelines. As the *Discipline* states, "Experience authenticates in our own lives the truths revealed in Scripture and illumined in tradition, enabling us to claim the Christian witness as our own."

TWO CHALLENGES

There are two significant challenges to this chapter. First, experience is often a very personal, subjective matter, and this makes it difficult to generalize for purposes of discussion and debate. Each of the Wesleyan

Quadrilateral's other three sides has commonly accepted standards to assess and compare the positions that people hold. These standards allow for a critique of the quality of a biblical interpretation, the relevance of church tradition, and the soundness of a rational argument. It becomes much more difficult when one tries to assess the veracity and applicability of a personal experience. Who is to judge whether or not it was truly God's voice that I heard in the woods? Who is to say whether or not the Holy Spirit truly warmed John Wesley's heart? The subjective nature of personal experience makes objective analysis difficult.

The second challenge is the imbalance between progressives and traditionalists in their use of experience in the dispute over homosexuality. In each chapter, this book has provided equal consideration to both factions within the United Methodist Church, alternating back-and-forth between the two perspectives. However, this chapter reads a little differently because, when it comes to the issue of homosexuality, progressives invoke personal experience more often and more broadly than traditionalists. For LGBTQ people and their allies, sharing their personal experiences and proclaiming how these stories reveal God's loving grace and empowerment in their lives is a vital testament to the new life God is giving—new life for both them and the Church. Traditionalists undoubtedly have compelling stories of God's personal revelation in their lives as well, but they are often skeptical or critical of the ways progressives apply personal experiences to the homosexuality debate.

We see anecdotal evidence of this imbalance by visiting the websites of prominent traditionalist and progressive advocacy groups. For example, the site for the progressive Reconciling Ministries Network, an organization that promotes full inclusion of LGBTQ people in the United Methodist Church, features two ways to share personal experiences with the world. Their blog has a tag, "Sharing Your Story," where over 170 personal accounts are available to read. Also, the website recently initiated a video project entitled, "This is My Story: LGBTQ United Methodists Share Their Experiences," with a new video featured on Facebook each week. For both of these initiatives, Reconciling Ministries Network provides detailed guidelines on how to effectively communicate one's story.

Conversely, the websites of traditionalist organizations like Good News and the Wesleyan Covenant Association make no such concerted effort to gather and share personal experiences. The website of Transforming

Congregations, a smaller affiliate of Good News that promotes "sanctified and life-giving sexuality," has a page dedicated to sharing personal testimonies, but no testimonies are posted.

The framework of this chapter will reflect this disproportionate way that experience is used by progressives and traditionalists when deliberating homosexuality. The next section provides a detailed account of the personal experiences of LGBTQ people. These experiences lead progressives to conclude that LGBTQ identity and behavior are God-given gifts that the United Methodist Church should embrace. The chapter then explores the ways that traditionalists critique the progressive approach, finding fault with the overly-broad and overly-prominent manner in which progressives invoke personal experience to resist the church's restrictions on homosexuality.

The chapter offers a less extensive analysis of the ways personal experiences are utilized by traditionalists, including a similarly concise progressive critique of the traditionalist approach. The relative attention given to these subjects is consistent with the way the theological tool of experience has been used by United Methodists when addressing the topic of homosexuality.

The chapter also includes an overview of some key moments when pastors chose to publicly defy the policies of the United Methodist Church, and it investigates how the church responded to these defiant acts of conscience. The chapter concludes with an overview of the divergent ways progressives and traditionalists interpret the work of the Holy Spirit.

LGBTQ EXPERIENCES

The personal experiences of LGBTQ people and their progressive allies play a prominent role in the formation of their theological views. Examples of this can be seen in the recent book, *Our Strangely Warmed Hearts*, by Karen Oliveto, the first openly LGBTQ person to ever serve as a bishop in the United Methodist Church. It is telling that Oliveto devoted the entire second half of her book to first-hand accounts of ten LGBTQ persons who represent a diverse and wide swath of the United Methodist Church. It is also noteworthy that she titles this section, "Coming Out as an Experience of God's Grace," further emphasizing the significance of experience to the theological beliefs of progressives. Oliveto introduces these personal accounts by declaring that we as a denomination have failed to look for the fruits of the Spirit in the lives of LGBTQ persons, and thus we "invalidate their personal relationships with Jesus Christ."

While it is unwise to assume that this small collection of stories fully captures the spiritual experiences of all LGBTQ persons, it nevertheless can offer a general sense of the experiences many lesbian and gay people have. This section briefly summarizes some spiritual themes embedded in the narratives that LGBTQ people share in *Our Strangely Warmed Hearts*, namely remaining in the closet; marginalization by the church; coming out; acceptance and affirmation; and resistance and action.[1]

Remaining in the Closet

Many LGBTQ individuals in the United Methodist Church, especially clergy, are hesitant to reveal their sexual identity and thus they remain in the proverbial closet. Thomas Carney says that there are many reasons to stay closeted. Ministering at the same church for 34 years, he withheld his sexual orientation because he wanted to be viewed simply as a pastor and not as a gay pastor. Also, he notes that there is still a danger to coming out, including the attitudes of some "good church folk" who want to see LGBTQ people either dismissed from the church or "cured" of their sexual desires.

Several individuals, including Deborah Morgan, mention that the church's implicit "don't ask, don't tell" policy was the "only viable option" if she and her partner were to serve as ministry leaders. Kay Knowlton and Barbara Lee reflect, "The necessity to be closeted in the church in order to be respected and accepted has been a deeply conflicting experience." JJ McCane notes that people expend a tremendous amount of energy hiding their LGBTQ identity, and Jarrell Wilson expresses incredulity at the need to remain closeted while hearing church members make hostile comments about LGBTQ individuals and allies. Keeping one's sexual identity confidential takes its toll on a person, and several stories include confessions of suicidal thoughts that accompany the pressure of maintaining the deep-seated secret of one's sexual identity.

---

1 The complete narratives of each person can be found in Karen Oliveto, *Our Strangely Warmed Hearts*, 67-128.

Marginalization by the Church

An unmistakable recurring theme in the stories of LGBTQ people is the deep pain and sorrow they experience within the church. Jarrell Wilson states bluntly, "Queer people aren't safe in The UMC, we aren't welcomed, and we aren't loved here." Kay Knowlton and Barbara Lee express anguish over both the church's "benign neglect" of LGBTQ persons and its official policies on homosexuality. They lament, "For our lives to be described as 'incompatible with Christian teaching' was devastating."

Thomas Carney remembers the fear he experienced because of the anti-gay rhetoric he heard at supposedly Christian conferences. Acknowledging that the church also offers positive care and support, Carney states, "The church of Jesus Christ was plunging a dagger in me and at the same time applying the salve."

Such marginalizing experiences prompted Deborah Morgan to feel embarrassed about belonging to a denomination that would do such harm to gay and lesbian people. She believes that future generations will judge this era harshly, finding it inconceivable that we presently mistreat LGBTQ people with such malice. Several times Morgan asked God to allow her to leave the United Methodist Church, even though she had a powerful, life-changing encounter with Jesus as a teenager. She would have parted with the denomination if not for the influence of her partner Gayle.

Coming Out

Elyse Ambrose notes that coming out to others is an intensely personal experience that must be done carefully, strategically, and only with the prompting of the Holy Spirit. The accounts of revealing one's LGBTQ identity to others vary widely—various contexts, various motivations, and various responses. Some chose to come out fully and decisively, while others preferred a more cautious, partial approach. However, virtually all the stories of coming out involve a shift from living a secretive and destructive way to experiencing a new and liberating authenticity.

Oneida C. is an instructive example. While many LGBTQ people experience immediate acceptance and affirmation upon coming out, others like Oneida initially experienced rejection and marginalization.

When she decided to come out, she was abandoned by her friends and isolated by her church. Her mother despised her, remarking that having cancer would be a preferable fate. Oneida thought she would need to make a choice between loving herself and loving her God. However, during a tough and lonely time while staying at a hostel, she experienced the warm, comforting, assuring presence of God. The next day, Oneida met a woman who identified as both gay and Christian. This woman attended an affirming United Methodist congregation, and hearing about this woman's spiritual journey helped Oneida realize that she, too, could have her spiritual well filled.

As powerful and positive as coming-out experiences are, Elyse Ambrose emphasizes that coming out to the church, to family, and to friends were not the most important experiences for her. Instead, "it was coming out to myself in the presence of God.... There I had to find God in myself and love her fiercely."

Acceptance and Affirmation

The stories in *Our Strangely Warmed Hearts* typically have specific moments when, upon revealing their LGBTQ identity, people feel an overwhelming sense of acceptance from others and from God. Sometimes this acceptance is immediate, while other times the acceptance only comes later. When JJ McCane decided to come out, each person she told offered her "safety, acceptance, support, and love." They affirmed her God-given gifts and her call to ministry. When her parents responded with similar grace, she found herself in the arms of Christ as the heavy burden of silence was lifted. McCane exclaims, "The door of the closet has forever been removed as I am confident in my identity and my call to ministry," and she hopes to share the unconditional love of God with others.

Oneida C. experienced God's grace by worshiping, studying, and fellowshipping with other LGBTQ persons, including a group of gay and lesbian Christians who are also Asian Pacific Islanders. Deborah Morgan similarly experienced a liberating love and acceptance at the hospital where she served as chaplain, and also with United Methodists who were part of the Reconciling Ministries Network.

Sean Delmore came out as gay (but continued to conceal his transgender identity) to his high school classmates and teachers in a very formal, public setting. Immediately upon doing so, he experienced a warm glow in his chest as a "gentle chant whispered through my veins: 'You are loved. You are loved.'" While difficult to believe at first, this moment began a journey of deeper commitment to Christ.

Resistance and Action

The personal decision about how one should advocate for change is a struggle for many LGBTQ people. Some, like Thomas Carney, focus on their local congregational ministries. Others are more like Rose, who feels called by God to advocate for justice, yet at the same time made the painful but prudent decision not to protest at the 2016 General Conference in front of her bishop.

LGBTQ people often interpret their experiences of struggle and discrimination as opportunities to serve God, promote justice, and transform the world. Israel Alvaran, a gay pastor from the Philippines, is thankful for his sexual identity because it has helped him to identify with those who are subjugated and to fight against systems of oppression.

A strong recurring theme in the stories of LGBTQ people is the ability to help others who have been relegated to the margins of society. Elyse Ambrose, a black queer woman, announced that she came out to let her LGBTQ siblings know that they are not alone and that she stands with them. Oneida C. and her spouse share their story with others to help mentor young queer Christians, empower LGBTQ allies, and express their love for marginalized communities.

Deborah Morgan and her spouse Gayle Felton devoted themselves to changing the United Methodist Church through the formal channels of church policy and order. However, as Felton neared death and realized that she would not see her denomination change its position on homosexuality in her lifetime, she confided to her spouse that perhaps the next generation will need to engage in "methods of open disobedience and disruption."

Oliveto's Conclusion

Bishop Oliveto closes *Our Strangely Warmed Hearts* with a plea to see the grace of God in the experiences of LGBTQ people. She expresses despair over the way the United Methodist Church has "veered from its love ethic and grace-filled theology, failing to recognize the way God's love and grace is moving in the lives of its LGBTQ members." Oliveto further recalls presiding over "too many funerals of LGBTQ persons who could not bear the pain the church has inflicted on them." She further recalls the saddest pastoral visit that she ever made, when a gay man asked her to "unbaptize" him, "because he had heard the stance of The UMC regarding LGBTQ people and felt he was no longer worthy of God's love and claim on his life." Oliveto later adds, "As long as the lives of LGBTQ persons are reduced to an 'issue,' it is easy to discount the movement of the Holy Spirit in their lives."

Bishop Oliveto concludes her book with a word of hope. No matter what the future holds for the church, "God will continue to work in the lives of LGBTQ persons who have been raised in the church, have encountered the Christ through its ministries, and who have responded to the call, 'Come, follow me.'"

TRADITIONALIST CRITIQUE

For LGBTQ individuals and their allies, the experiences described in the previous section provide evidence of God's affirming grace in the lives of gay and lesbian people, and it also demonstrates God's transformation of the church into a more loving and inclusive Body of Christ. Traditionalists, however, contend that progressives are misunderstanding and misusing the theological tool of experience, suggesting that their errant application comes in two forms. First, traditionalists fault progressives for defining experience much more broadly than the Wesleyan tradition has historically understood it. Second, traditionalists believe that progressives have made experience too prominent in their theological thinking, even to the point of privileging it above Scripture. Below is a more thorough exploration of these two critiques.

Making Experience Too Broad

Scholar Bill Arnold reflects the traditionalist view when he says that personal experience has a particular and limited purpose. He says that John Wesley intended experience to serve as a confirmation of the foundational truths revealed in Scripture and tradition. In the context of the Wesleyan Quadrilateral, then, experience plays a subservient role. Arnold supports his position by quoting Albert Outler, the scholar who coined the term "Wesleyan Quadrilateral." Outler states, "Christian experience adds nothing to the substance of Christian truth; its distinctive role is to energize the heart so as to enable the believer to speak and do the truth in love."[2]

Because experience plays a subordinate role in theological reflection, it encompasses a very limited purview for traditionalists. For them, experience is confined specifically to the experience of Christian assurance, the confirmation of God's justifying and saving grace in one's life. The quintessential example of such experience is Wesley's Aldersgate experience. During a prolonged crisis of faith in which Wesley doubted his salvation, he reluctantly attended a society meeting where someone was reading from Martin Luther's preface to the book of Romans. During a description of "the change which God works in the heart through faith," Wesley recounted in his journal:

> I felt my heart strangely warmed. I felt I did trust in Christ, Christ alone for salvation; and an assurance was given me that He had taken away my sins, even mine, and saved me from the law of sin and death.

For the traditionalist, this is the precise role of experience in the life of a Christian—a personal confirmation of God's redemption and salvation. Wesleyan scholar Kevin Watson asserts that "the role of experience in Wesley's theology, then, is quite particular. It is not any experience that a person has, it is the distinctively Christian experience of assurance of the forgiveness of one's sins."[3]

Thus, traditionalists are critical of the expanded role of experience typically granted by progressives. Progressives are more likely to value a full spectrum of human experiences as evidence of God's love. It is not a coincidence that Bishop Oliveto titled her LGBTQ-affirming book *Our Strangely Warmed Hearts*. She and other progressives typically equate

---

2 Quoted in Bill Arnold, *Seeing Black and White in a Gray World*, 90.

3 Kevin Watson, "Experience in the So-Called 'Wesleyan Quadrilateral.'"

their inner assurance of God's affirmation of their LGBTQ identity with the inner assurance of God's salvation that John Wesley experienced at Aldersgate. Traditionalists, however, insist that these are two very different types of experiences, and only the latter is an appropriate application of experience as intended by the Wesleyan Quadrilateral.

Scholar Donald Thorsen makes a traditionalist argument when he warns that all experience, even religious experience, is subjective, ambiguous, easily distorted, potentially deceptive, and open to multiple interpretations. Because of this, Thorsen contends, "Experience properly construed is interpreted in the light of biblical revelation." Applied specifically to the debate over LGBTQ issues, he states:

> The problem with the homosexuality debates today is that the "testimonies" of some gay and lesbian Christians are considered self-authenticating. The rationalization or acceptance of their behavior is deemed to be valid just because that is what they are experiencing. *What is* becomes confused with *what ought to be*—the normative (emphasis in the original).[4]

Making Experience Too Prominent

Traditionalists further insist that the expanded use of experience by progressives leads to a reversal in the proper hierarchy of the Wesleyan Quadrilateral. Specifically, traditionalists criticize progressives for making experience equally important—or perhaps even more important—than Scripture. A striking example of this comes from prominent scholar Luke Timothy Johnson, who teaches at a United Methodist seminary. Johnson expresses impatience for modern-day efforts to interpret the Bible in ways that negate the obvious condemnations of homosexual behavior. He then contends:

> We must state our grounds for standing in tension with the clear commands of Scripture.... I think it important to state clearly that we do, in fact, reject the straightforward commands of Scripture, and appeal instead to another authority when we declare that same-sex

---

4 Donald Thorsen, "John Wesley, Revelation, and Homosexual Experience."

unions can be holy and good. And what exactly is that authority? We appeal explicitly to the weight of our own experience and the experience thousands of others have witnessed to, which tells us that to claim our own sexual orientation is in fact to accept the way in which God has created us.[5]

For the traditionalist, such a declaration is wholly unacceptable. It privileges a subjective and overly-broad understanding of experience over and above Holy Scripture, the primary and authoritative source of religious truth for Methodists throughout their history. Traditionalists suspect that such an inversion of the Wesleyan Quadrilateral's hierarchy is not limited to Johnson's views, but instead is endemic to the progressive perspective.

Kevin Watson believes that United Methodists must clarify the way in which the Wesleyan Quadrilateral is used within the denomination. A choice must be made between the traditional usage as originally outlined by Outler (who later expressed regret over the way his Quadrilateral had become distorted) and the progressive usage of it. Watson declares:

> If Methodists are going to continue citing the quadrilateral as their distinctive theological method, then we have a choice to make. We can return to an understanding of experience as it was defined by Outler in his creation of the quadrilateral. Or, we can knowingly reject the way that he defined experience as a legitimate source for Christian theology and use it in a way that he explicitly rejected. If we choose the latter, we ought to at least be honest that we are now using a method of theological reflection that neither John Wesley nor Albert Outler would have endorsed.[6]

TRADITIONALIST EXPERIENCES

Stories of traditionalists grappling with homosexuality are not as widespread as progressive stories. When traditionalists do recount such experiences, they often focus on choice—either choosing to be heterosexual or choosing to remain celibate.

---

5 Luke Timothy Johnson, "Homosexuality & the Church."

6 Kevin Watson, "Experience in the So-Called 'Wesleyan Quadrilateral.'"

Choosing to be Heterosexual

In some instances, individuals who experience same-sex attraction choose not to embrace a lesbian or gay identity but instead make a conscious choice to live a heterosexual life. Susan McDonald is one such person. In the 2003 traditionalist anthology *Staying the Course*, McDonald recounts the moment when she went to the microphone as a delegate at her California-Pacific Annual Conference. After witnessing a skit that clearly implied homosexuality was an inborn characteristic, McDonald decided to expose a long-held secret before 1,000 other delegates. After chastising the bishop for wearing a rainbow ribbon on his collar, she announced, "Bishop, I stand before you as someone who lived as a lesbian for nearly ten years. I have left that lifestyle behind me and have been free of it for over 20 years now. How dare you permit people to propagate the lie that 'I can't change.'"[7]

McDonald decided to speak out because of her swelling indignation regarding the increased acceptance of homosexuality that she was witnessing in her progressive-leaning annual conference. "In the middle of all the controversy," she writes, "I came to the realization that no one was saying what I knew to be true—that many, many people can and do choose to leave the gay lifestyle." McDonald suggests that stories of such decisions are seemingly sparse because people like her are unwilling to speak out. "The truth is that those of us who have left the lifestyle (and the stigma it carries) behind are unwilling to stand and confess it. And so our silence leaves only the activists' voices incessantly drilling the same untruths into the public ear."

Looking back at her time as a lesbian in her twenties, McDonald calls this decade "the most horrible period of my life." Keeping her lesbian behavior a secret, she left her marriage, surrendered custody of her young child, and lived in constant fear and anxiety of having her secret exposed. She contemplated suicide many times. But McDonald turned to the Lord, and eventually her life—and her sexuality—turned around.

McDonald recalls, "It took a long time for me to realize that it wasn't true that I had to be gay." She was prepared to remain celibate, "but I was not going to continue the way I had been." After turning to the

---

7 Susan McDonald, "Lesbian No More," in *Staying the Course*, eds. Dunnam and Malony, 170-174.

Lord, she experienced restoration in her family relationships. Ultimately, McDonald says, "I met and married a church-going man. God restored the wasted years." She sees her time of struggle as preparation to minister to others, and she gives an earnest plea to gay and lesbian people, "I can say to people who are currently trapped in the gay lifestyle, 'It isn't true that you can't change!' You are one of God's special, loved children, and *you have a choice!* My own life is the truth of what I tell you." (emphasis in original)

When progressives hear such stories, it typically conjures up images of reparative therapy in which LGBTQ people are compelled to change their inherent orientation. They emphasize that professional organizations such as the American Psychiatric Association and the American Psychological Association denounce such practices. Religiously, progressives contend that choosing heterosexuality when one is LGBTQ is tantamount to denying the way that God created them.

Choosing to Remain Celibate

The *Book of Discipline* states that ordained pastors must exhibit "celibacy in singleness." Because the *Discipline* also says that the practice of homosexuality is incompatible with Christian teaching, traditionalists contend that remaining single and celibate is an appropriate recourse for those who experience same-sex attraction. The accounts below highlight the experiences of two men who made the choice to remain celibate.

Christopher Adams. Christopher Adams proclaims that, at age 44, he was born again. "Over the course of several days, the Holy Spirit swept over me like a flood."[8] This transformative experience resulted in Adams's decision to remain celibate as a gay man.

Raised in a small and loving church in rural North Carolina, Adams was 17 when he admitted to himself that he was gay. While avoiding any definitive explanation for his same-sex attraction, Adams is confident that he "never would have chosen to be gay—it only makes life harder, and I had no desire to marginalize myself." He is grateful that his mother was "cautiously supportive" and that his extended family was "politely tolerant" when he told them that he was gay.

---

8 Christopher Adams, "Sharing in Faith: A View from Both Sides."

Leaving the church and opting for an entirely secular life, Adams met a long-term partner with whom he lived for six years. However, a few years ago, upon returning to his rural hometown to care for his elderly grandmother, Adams experienced a conversion. After years of spiritual emptiness, he has found "inexplicable peace" and experienced "the depth of God's love" while reading Scripture. "I believe that I've been looking for my father my entire life," Adams declares, "and over the last year I finally found Him."

Within this context, Adams declares, "I've made a conscious decision to be celibate." He isn't, however, trying to avoid being labeled a "practicing homosexual." Adams teases, "When I first read that term last year, I thought, 'I don't have to practice any more. By now I'm a professional.'" The core motivation for his celibacy, says Adams, is "allowing myself some holy space while sorting through what I believe about my own sexual orientation and the nature of sin."

Adams is not a conventional traditionalist. He confesses to being "deeply conflicted" over the issue of same-sex marriage. He supports it as a civil right (though he would prefer it be called a "civil union"), and he respects the desire and sincerity of Christian same-sex couples who seek to change the denomination's restrictions. He confesses, "At times I feel like a traitor or a hypocrite for leaning toward the conservative side of this debate." Adams continues, "When I think of same-sex couples I know who have been together for 40 or 50 years (yes, they exist), I can't imagine telling them they're excluded from the Kingdom unless they commit to celibacy." He understands that God can use the challenge and commitment of celibacy to draw people closer, but Adams also concedes that he is at a loss for solid answers.

Yet, for Adams personally, he opts to remain a celibate gay man. While "the thought of never falling in love again makes me sad," Adams nevertheless asserts, "for me, celibacy means embracing other men only in *philia* (brotherly love), not in *eros* (erotic love)."

Rob Renfroe's Colleague. United Methodist pastor Rob Renfroe is president of Good News and a prominent traditionalist leader. In his recent book, *Are We Really Better Together?* (with Walter Fenton), he discusses his church's response to a fellow pastor who experiences same-sex attraction but chooses to remain celibate:

I think it might surprise people to know that the church where I (Rob) serve as pastor of discipleship has had on staff a pastor who was open about his same-gender attraction. He was a powerful preacher, an incredibly loving presence, and a champion for being in ministry with the poor. We loved him and we still do. He was committed to celibacy because of his faith, and we saw no reason that his same-gender attraction should disqualify him from ordained ministry or from serving as a leader in our congregation. We were happy for his many contributions to the life of our church, and we were sad when he left us to do campus ministry.[9]

Renfroe emphasizes that the longstanding United Methodist stance on homosexuality, a position supported by traditionalists, focuses on sexual activity, not sexual desire. Renfroe continues:

You will never find us condemning anyone because he or she is attracted to persons of the same gender. One reason we can affirm the United Methodist position is because it does not condemn or shame persons for their feelings or their attractions, but rather calls us to control our actions.

PASTORAL ACTS OF CONSCIENCE

The *Book of Discipline* states (¶105) that Christian experience "illumines our understanding of God and creation and motivates us to make sensitive moral judgments." Sometimes United Methodist pastors make moral judgments that call into question the standard practices of the church. These acts of conscience then become legal issues that the church must address. Below are several brief accounts of times when pastors challenged church law regarding homosexuality, and thus faced judicial consequences from the denomination. With one exception, the accounts are from landmark cases involving progressive pastors who were challenging the church's positions on same-sex marriage and the ordination of gay and lesbian clergy.

---

9 Rob Renfroe and Walter Fenton, *Are We Really Better Together?*, 45.

Defrocking (Jimmy Creech)

In 1997, Jimmy Creech, a respected United Methodist pastor in Nebraska, presided over a covenant service for two women. Charges were filed against him, and a church trial was held to determine if Creech had violated the *Book of Discipline*'s prohibition of officiating same-sex weddings. The 1996 *Discipline* clearly states (¶65), "Ceremonies that celebrate homosexual unions shall not be conducted by our ministers and shall not be conducted in our churches." However, Creech's defense argued that, because this statement is found in the Social Principles section, it should be treated more as an instructive guideline that does not rise to the level of church law like other sections of the *Discipline*. This defense was effective, and Creech was acquitted of the charges.

However, a year later in August 1998, the United Methodist Judicial Council ruled that the Social Principles' prohibition of homosexual unions did, indeed, "have the force of church law." Thus, Creech was again placed on trial in 1999 after he co-officiated a second covenant service in April of that year, this time for two men. Creech's bishop had given him explicit instructions to cease from officiating any more same-sex union ceremonies.

During this second trial, Creech defended his defiance of a church decree by asserting that "the law was unjust and the whole trial is corrupted." In his closing statement, Creech appealed to the jury of his clerical peers by proclaiming:

> You have been asked to uphold a law which is wrong. You are about to do something that is unjust and violent. The priority as a Christian puts our call above injury, harm and suffering. Such causes violence against our brothers and sisters. We are called to be beloved in the United Methodist Church.[10]

Riley Case, a member of the traditionalist Confessing Movement who was attending the trial, rebuffed Creech's contention that church law should be disobeyed because of a presumed higher law:

> There is a great deal of arrogance [in Creech's argument], because Scripture and 2,000 years of church history—that are in all Christian denominations in all countries—has been

---

10 Trial quotes in this section are from Daniel Gangler, "Creech Found Guilty."

disregarded. Creech renders invalid everything taught about truth of faithfulness in marriage and celibacy in singleness. All of this is in jeopardy if we are to follow the plea of Jimmy Creech.

The jury's decision was unanimous: Creech had violated church law, and thus his ministerial credentials should be revoked. Jimmy Creech was no longer a United Methodist pastor.

Refusing Membership (Ed Johnson)

Ed Johnson pastored a United Methodist Church in Virginia. When an active participant at the church approached him about becoming a full member in 2004, Johnson declined his request, citing the individual's "homosexual orientation and practice." Johnson's district superintendent instructed Johnson that he was required to accept and receive anyone who sincerely makes the membership vows. When Johnson continued to decline, the district superintendent filed charges against him. After lengthy deliberations and legal proceedings, Johnson was placed on an involuntary leave of absence.

Johnson appealed to Judicial Council, the highest court in United Methodism. His legal counsel argued that Johnson was using appropriate pastoral discernment when he refused membership to the gay man. They further argued that the pastor of a local church congregation has the authority to determine such decisions. Noting that the focus of Johnson's refusal of membership was the man's homosexual practice, not identity, Johnson's lawyer stated, "The pastor felt that the person was not able to take that vow, because he did not honestly acknowledge that his practice was a sin."[11]

The Judicial Council sided with Johnson, declaring "The pastor in charge of a United Methodist church or charge is solely responsible for making the determination of a person's readiness to receive the vows of membership." The Council further added that "a pastor-in-charge cannot be ordered by the district superintendent or bishop" to admit a person into membership. The Council viewed the case as a question about a pastor's authority, not a matter of membership status for LGBTQ people.

---

11 Details of Johnson's story are from Alan Cooperman, "Case of Gay Worshiper in Va. Splits Methodists."

However, in her dissenting opinion, Judicial Council member Susan Henry-Crowe remarked that the decision "compromises the historical understanding that the Church is open to all."

Traditionalists viewed the judicial ruling as a victory not only for the traditional values of the church but also for the rule and order of church law. Conversely, the decision caused great concern among progressives, who worried that this decision would lead to further marginalization and exclusion of LGBTQ people from other congregations throughout the denomination. In the ensuing years, Judicial Council has been repeatedly petitioned to reconsider this decision, but each time it has declined.

Self-Avowals (Karen Dammann and Beth Stroud)

In 2004, two lesbian pastors, Karen Dammann of Seattle and Beth Stroud of Philadelphia, each made independent public proclamations of their sexual identity, and both proclamations became matters of national interest.

Karen Dammann. Pastor Karen Dammann decided to disclose to her bishop that she was "living in a partnered, covenanted homosexual relationship" with her long-term partner.[12] They decided to make this pronouncement to the bishop after an incident when a church supervisor was planning to visit their home. Dammann insisted that her partner scrape a gay-rights bumper sticker off her car to conceal their sexual orientation. Upon realizing the lengths they were going to hide their sexual identities, Dammann and her partner decided that such secrecy was sending the wrong message to their five-year-old son.

Upon learning of her sexuality, Dammann's bishop filed formal charges. Dammann was the second pastor in United Methodist history to be placed on trial for being a self-avowed practicing homosexual. The only previous trial had been 17 years earlier when Rose Mary Denman was found guilty and defrocked in 1987.

Dammann's trial, however, had a different result, at least initially. By a vote of 11-0 (with two abstentions), she was cleared of all charges. The jury of 13 pastors contended that, while the *Book of Discipline* states that

---

12 Details of Dammann's story are from Matthew Preusch and Laurie Goodstein, "Jury of Methodists Clears Gay Minister Over a Relationship."

homosexual practice is "incompatible" with Christian teaching, it does not outright bar LGBTQ people from serving as pastors.

Traditionalists were incredulous toward the ruling. Maxie Dunnam, president of Asbury Theological Seminary, exclaimed, "How can there be a not guilty verdict when what she's done is public and she has confessed it? I'm very surprised and I'm very disappointed because it's another sign of really anarchy in the church."

The progressive victory was to be short-lived. President Dunnam and other traditionalists petitioned Judicial Council to review the decision. Although Judicial Council determined that it had no authority to overturn the verdict of the previous trial, they also ruled that church law prohibits a bishop from appointing a self-avowed practicing homosexual to a ministerial position. In effect, the jury verdict of Karen Dammann's trial determined that she remained eligible to serve as a minister, but her self-disclosure during the trial proceedings had disqualified her from ever again being appointed as a pastor in the United Methodist Church.

Beth Stroud. "I have come to a place where my discipleship, my walk with Christ, requires telling the whole truth and paying whatever price truthfulness requires." So stated Beth Stroud as she publicly announced her lesbian orientation from the pulpit during an Easter-season sermon in 2003.[13] This was hardly news to Stroud's supportive congregation, many of whom were aware of Stroud's long-term same-sex relationship. However, this self-avowal now made Stroud vulnerable to formal charges that jeopardized her clergy status.

In December 2004, Stroud faced a church trial with a jury of her pastoral peers. By a vote of 12-1, Stroud was found guilty of violating the *Book of Discipline*'s prohibition of non-celibate gay and lesbian clergy. This was a dramatically different outcome from Karen Dammann's 11-0 not-guilty vote at her trial. One possible reason for this difference may be that, during the months between these two trials, the Judicial Council made a new ruling that public declarations of homosexual practice are officially a chargeable offense for United Methodist ministers.

A year later, the Judicial Council upheld the original jury vote of Stroud's trial. Stroud was defrocked of her United Methodist clergy

---

13 Details of Stroud's story are from Alan Cooperman, "Gay Minister to Face Jury of Methodist Peers" and "Lesbian Minister Defrocked by United Methodist Church."

credentials, though her church continued to hire her as a lay minister for several years after the decision. Stroud reflected, "If it's a choice between serving in the ordained ministry with my credentials intact, and serving as an 'out' lesbian person acknowledging the most important relationship in my life and not having those credentials, I'll take being out. I think it's better and more honest, and more healthy in the long run."

"A Moment of Reformation" (Amy DeLong)

In 2009, two women asked Wisconsin pastor Amy DeLong to officiate their Holy Union. Although these women (Carrie and Carolyn) had left the church because of its treatment of LGBTQ people, they still wanted God represented at their ceremony. DeLong agreed, and her supporters later exclaimed, "From outside the church came the impetus to reform the church. Like the Holy Spirit at Pentecost, Carrie and Carolyn began to break open a closed-in church fearful of those who spoke a different language, who had a different sexual orientation."[14]

When DeLong disclosed in her annual report that she presided over a same-sex ceremony, it triggered a series of complaints and deliberations over the event. DeLong thought it odd that the grievances focused on the same-sex ceremony but not her own sexual orientation, so during this process she further disclosed that she was a lesbian living in a legal domestic partnership. Ultimately, DeLong was formally charged and brought to trial both for celebrating a same-sex union and for being a "self-avowed practicing homosexual."

The trial in the progressive-leaning Wisconsin Annual Conference had a historic outcome. Despite her acknowledgment of being a lesbian in a committed relationship, the clergy jury dismissed the charge of being a self-avowed practicing homosexual because DeLong refused to answer any explicit questions about her sexual activity. However, the jury unanimously found DeLong guilty of officiating a same-sex ceremony. But rather than defrocking her, the jury levied a much lighter sentence—a 20-day suspension and a requirement to draft a document that would outline procedures to more harmoniously resolve issues that harm the clergy covenant and create an adversarial spirit.

14 "Trial Summary."

The ruling was historic because it was the first time in over 20 years that a pastor was not defrocked when found guilty of officiating a homosexual union. DeLong's support team rejoiced, declaring, "We have experienced another moment of resurrection, restitution, reformation and renewal." Traditionalist Rob Renfroe, however, objected to the decision. Calling it a "slap on the wrist," he remarked, "In no other institution in the world would we see such a ludicrous response."[15] He further suggested that no other organization, religious or secular, would allow an individual "to break its policies and embarrass it publicly simply because you believe you are more enlightened or more sincere than it is."

"Biblical Obedience" (Melvin Talbert)

"I stand before you here this afternoon and I declare that God has already settled this matter: all human beings are created in the image of God. There are no exceptions, no exclusions. We belong to the family of God." These words were spoken by retired Bishop Melvin Talbert at a gathering on the final day of the 2004 General Conference.[16] When the conference yet again maintained the traditionalist restrictions on same-sex behavior, Talbert made a contentious proclamation: "I declare to you that the derogatory language and restrictive laws in the *Book of Discipline* are immoral and unjust and no longer deserve our loyalty and obedience."

A lifelong proponent of civil rights, Talbert was on stage with 14 other bishops (8 retired, 6 active) when he made the pronouncement. He further encouraged others to engage in what he called "biblical obedience": "I call on the clergy who have signed the pledge [to resist LGBTQ restrictions] to stand firm in their resolve to perform marriages among same-sex couples and to do so in the normal course of their pastoral duties." Not only did Talbert encourage pastors to ignore the prohibition to officiate same-sex weddings, he further pressed for churches to open their sanctuaries for such events, which is also banned by the *Discipline*.

For many progressives, this experience was a sacred moment. David Meredith, a pastor and board member of the Reconciling Ministries Network, declared:

---

15 Rob Renfroe, "The DeLong Challenge."

16 Details in this section are from Lois McCullen Parr, "Bishop Talbert: A Call for Biblical Obedience."

In the Tampa Tabernacle [where Talbert made his proclamation], the people of God encountered the Divine Presence today. Like the Tabernacle of scripture, a people wandering for 40 years in the wilderness of unjust law, immoral teaching, and dehumanizing actions toward LGBT persons experienced the presence of God.

Soon after, Talbert stayed true to his words and officiated a same-sex wedding near Birmingham, Alabama. He did so despite the local bishop's request that he refrain from this controversial and potentially divisive act. Formal charges were made against Talbert, both for his public proclamation to defy the *Book of Discipline* and for his officiating of a same-sex wedding.

Through a series of deliberations with other bishops, the charges were resolved before Talbert faced trial. Talbert expressed regret for the "felt harm and unintended consequences" that his actions caused, but he held steadfastly to "the conviction that his actions were just and right." Traditionalists like Tom Lambrecht, vice president of Good News, decried the lack of accountability in the resolution, stating, "The perception will surely be left that a bishop can violate the church's teachings with impunity and suffer no consequences whatsoever when it comes to same-sex services. It's a sad day for the church."[17]

CONCLUSION: INVOKING THE HOLY SPIRIT

Gracie Allen, the famous vaudevillian and early-television comedian, once quipped, "Never place a period where God has placed a comma." Christian experience testifies that God's work has not ended, but instead remains active in our personal lives, in the church, and in the world. Likewise, Scripture declares that God is always doing a new thing, always transforming God's people into a new creation (Isaiah 43:19, 65:17; 2 Corinthians 5:17; Revelation 21:5). The Holy Spirit is still moving, still shaping, still transforming. And yet, when it comes to the matter of homosexuality, progressives and traditionalists have markedly divergent understandings of how the Holy Spirit is moving in the lives of God's people and in the United Methodist Church.

---

17 Walter Fenton, "No Consequences for Talbert's Defiance."

For progressives, the Holy Spirit is doing a new thing by eradicating the oppression and marginalization of LGBTQ people. The Spirit is making a new path that fully includes people of all sexual identities in the life of the church. The progressive celebration of the Spirit's action is evident in the ebullient way they describe the milestone election and consecration of Bishop Karen Oliveto, a married lesbian and first-ever openly LGBTQ person to serve as a bishop in the United Methodist Church. Kent Ingram and Emily Allen, two delegates at the 2016 Western Jurisdiction Conference where Bishop Oliveto was elected, effused, "It's hard to put into words the spiritual presence that we felt. The Holy Spirit had swept across the room; its power and presence real and obvious. It was a sacred moment on holy ground."[18]

Similarly, the Reconciling Ministries Network pronounced, "Who can deny that the Spirit has produced such fruit through the election and ministry of Bishop Oliveto? Who would dare stand in the way of God's work of producing fruit?" Reconciling Ministries also expressed concern over the prospect that Judicial Council could remove Oliveto as bishop because she is a self-avowed practicing homosexual. The group asserted, "To remove or prohibit Bishop Oliveto from her ministry as bishop would stand in the way of the Spirit's works as evidenced by the fruits we have seen in the church, we have heard in the stories of individuals, and we have known in our own hearts." For progressives, all of this is evidence that "the church has made itself one step closer to the life God intends for it."[19]

Reflecting on these progressive proclamations, traditionalist Walter Fenton casts doubt on the belief that Bishop Oliveto's election is truly the work of the Holy Spirit. Fenton asks, "What one of us does not want to invoke the Holy Spirit as the guiding power behind our cherished plans and hopes for the future?" He then notes that traditionalists have a sharply different understanding of the Spirit's movement in the United Methodist Church:

> For just as the Western Jurisdiction delegates claim the Holy Spirit "swept across" its meeting in Scottsdale, so a global and

---

18 "A Message to The United Methodist Church."
19 "No Such Law."

diverse church claims the Holy Spirit was guiding its deliberations and decisions at General Conference. It received no word from the Holy Spirit compelling it to overturn its sexual ethics and teachings on marriage. Instead, it heard just the opposite: the Holy Spirit's reaffirmation or reconfirmation of ethics and teachings rooted in Scripture and 2,000 years of church history.[20]

Traditionalists dismiss the suggestion that the Spirit is transforming the church to embrace a new sexual ethic. Instead, they believe that God is changing hearts and minds to faithfully resist cultural pressures and to exhibit the personal holiness that is required by both Holy Scriptures and Church tradition.

We thus see two sharply contradictory views of the Holy Spirit's work in the United Methodist Church. One believes the Spirit is radically transforming the denomination's stance toward homosexuality, while the other is confident that the Spirit is calling the church to preserve its historic teachings. With such diametrically opposed viewpoints, United Methodists are struggling to follow Paul's exhortation in his letter to the Ephesians (4:2b-3) to remain unified in the Holy Spirit: "Accept each other with love, and make an effort to preserve the unity of the Spirit with the peace that ties you together."

---

20 Walter Fenton, "Invoking the Holy Spirit."

QUESTIONS TO CONSIDER

Consider the following questions. If you are discussing in a group, commit to a respectful dialogue in which the goal is hearing and understanding one another rather than winning and advancing a particular point of view.

1. What personal experiences have significantly impacted your Christian faith? How did these experiences shape you? Have any personal experiences influenced your moral and theological understanding of homosexuality? If yes, what were these experiences and how did they shape your thinking?

2. Why do you think progressives emphasize experience more than traditionalists, particularly regarding matters related to homosexuality? Does this say anything about how these two groups understand their Wesleyan heritage and the Wesleyan Quadrilateral?

3. Reviewing the summary of LGBTQ experiences in this chapter, are there any stories or themes that you find especially striking or important? If so, which ones, and why? Which aspects of their stories do you find most compelling regarding the debate over homosexuality?

4. Do you agree with the traditionalist critique that progressives apply the theological task of homosexuality too broadly and too prominently? Is either of these a more significant critique than the other to you? If so, which one, and why? Which traditionalist arguments do you find most compelling regarding the debate over homosexuality?

5. Traditionalist experiences of same-sex desire emphasize choice, either the choice to be heterosexual or the choice to be celibate. Do you think these are appropriate responses for people who experience same-sex attraction? Why or why not?

6. Many progressive pastors have decided that, as an act of obedience to God's higher laws, it is a proper act of justice to disobey the policies and statutes of the United Methodist *Book of Discipline.* Do you think these are appropriate responses for clergy who disagree with the denomination's official positions? Why or why not?

7. Traditionalists and progressives have very different understandings of how the Holy Spirit is working in the individual and corporate lives of United Methodists. How do you think the Holy Spirit is moving regarding the controversy over homosexuality?

Chapter 5

REASON:
DIVIDED OVER EVIDENCE

THE POWER OF REASON

As I have mentioned in my previous reflections, I spent a good deal of my teenage and young adult years grappling with doubt. I found Jesus to be utterly compelling, and I considered myself a Christian, but how could I truly know that the claims of my faith are true?

While at college, I focused my studies on the sociology of knowledge, giving particular attention to religious knowledge. Using the tools of modern scholarship, I sought to understand the meaning of truth, and I also tried to grasp how various cultures determined what is true and what isn't. However, the more I sought answers, the more confused I often became. My sociological training left me wondering if I could ever depend on any knowledge to be entirely trustworthy, including the truth claims of my Christian faith.

The summer before leaving for graduate school, I worked as a youth leader for a United Methodist congregation. I befriended the associate pastor there, and he was intrigued that I aspired to become a sociology professor. One day he went to his bookshelf and said, "I have something for you." He pulled out a copy of *A Reasonable Faith* by Tony Campolo, an evangelical preacher who was also a sociology professor. "You might enjoy this," my pastor friend said, noting that Campolo and I shared the same academic discipline.

I did enjoy it. Written to communicate the Christian faith to a secular audience, *A Reasonable Faith* drew heavily from Campolo's sociological expertise, applying the ideas of sociological thinkers in ways that helped, rather than hindered, my Christian beliefs. I discovered a kindred spirit who had confronted virtually all of the same intellectual hurdles that I was encountering, and Campolo was providing answers that made sense to me. His book did not settle every matter for me, nor did it definitively prove the truth of Christianity's claims. It did, however, expose me to ideas and arguments that made the proclamations of the gospel message seem like a reasonable intellectual choice—a choice that I could embrace. My intellectual journey may have inflicted times of confusion and doubt, but my quest to rationally seek for truth ultimately strengthened my faith. The truth claims of the Bible became more real to me than ever before.

That's the power of reason.

UNITED METHODIST UNDERSTANDING OF REASON

I once had a poster of Jesus in my office. Beside the reverent medieval image of Christ, the poster read, "He died to take away your sins, not your mind."

This statement is consistent with a United Methodist understanding of reason. The *Book of Discipline* states (¶105), "Although we recognize that God's revelation and our experiences of God's grace continually surpass the scope of human language and reason, we also believe that any disciplined theological work calls for the careful use of reason." The *Discipline* goes on to list several appropriate applications of human reason, including reading and interpreting Scripture; determining the clarity of our Christian witness; and asking questions and seeking God's will.

A common saying about the relationship between biblical faith and human reason is that "all truth is God's truth." Such a view is affirmed by the United Methodist Church. "Since all truth is from God, efforts to discern the connections between revelation and reason, faith and science, grace and nature, are useful endeavors in developing credible and communicable doctrine." For the United Methodist, our capacity for logic, reason, rationality, and scientific inquiry are all God-given gifts that aid us as we try to discern and understand the biblical truths revealed in Scripture.

At the same time, we must approach reason with a sense of humility. The Apostle Paul warns us of the limits to human knowledge, declaring that we can only know things partially, as a reflection in a mirror. Only when we ultimately experience God face-to-face will we possess complete knowledge in the same way that God already thoroughly knows us: "Now we see a reflection in a mirror; then we will see face-to-face. Now I know partially, but then I will know completely in the same way that I have been completely known" (1 Corinthians 13:12). This humble approach to reason and rationality reminds us that we always have more to learn and that others may have insights that we haven't considered. Our knowledge *about* God can support, but it cannot replace, our faith and trust *in* God.

This chapter explores the ways United Methodists have applied reason to their understanding of homosexuality. Of course, reason has been interwoven throughout our previous examination of the other three prongs of the Wesleyan Quadrilateral. Biblical scholars use reason to study Scripture. Our Christian tradition is filled with thoughtful scholars and ministers carefully discerning how best to continue the legacy of the gospel. And devout women and men have always used their rational capacities to make sense of the influential and formative experiences in their lives. Although reason has been a backdrop for all of these other chapters, we now consider how intellectual inquiry has shaped our modern knowledge of same-sex relationships.

THE CHURCH STUDIES HOMOSEXUALITY

A Controversial Topic

Homosexuality is such a divisive issue in the United Methodist Church that even the seemingly harmless task of rationally investigating the topic has proven to be controversial. In 1976, early in the formation of the United Methodist Church, General Conference entertained a proposal to commission a denomination-wide study of human sexuality. Drawing upon the most recent scholarship, the study would be used to inform and equip the church. However, more than 1,400 petitions from around the United States flooded into the General Conference, objecting to such a study. Concerns over methodology, money, and motives ultimately brought down the proposal. Delegates instead approved a much weaker minority report recommending that local churches assume the task of studying human sexuality, but only if they chose to do so.

Advocates for a comprehensive study made similar proposals each quadrennium, but it was not until 1988 that General Conference eventually commissioned a comprehensive four-year study of human sexuality. The investigation would explore both theological and scientific questions, relying upon scholarly research from a broad spectrum of academic disciplines: theology, ethics, biology, psychology, sociology, and medicine. Delegates authorized the study committee to submit a report with recommendations for action at the 1992 General Conference in Louisville. As we shall see, reason and rationality do not guarantee a conclusive resolution to moral and religious debates.

Although the study was conducted more than a quarter-century ago, the findings of the committee and the response to the report are still telling and relevant today. It is helpful to see the types of issues the committee could agree upon, as well as those topics on which the committee remained divided. Below is a brief overview of the religious and scientific findings of the committee, and also the formal recommendations and the eventual outcome of this endeavor.

Findings

The Committee to Study Homosexuality was authorized to study homosexuality with the confidence that "the church possesses the resources of mind and spirit to resolve such issues reasonably and in faithfulness to the gospel it proclaims."[1] The study addressed both the theological and the scientific dimensions of homosexuality and provided General Conference with specific recommendations.

As the committee examined the biblical scholarship on homosexuality, they encountered many of the same conflicting interpretations that we saw in Chapter 2. Scholars did not agree on the meaning of the seven

---

1 Unless otherwise noted, details for this section are from *The Church Studies Homosexuality*.

scriptural passages that address same-sex behavior, nor did they concur on what can be learned about homosexuality from the biblical passages on creation and marriage. Likewise, the committee found no consensus among Christian ethicists regarding the morality of same-sex relations. Some ethicists regarded homosexual behavior as a grave moral vice, while others considered the issue to be of minor or no concern.

There was, however, widespread agreement that gay and lesbian individuals have been subjected to discrimination, stigmatization, and oppression, and that the Church has a responsibility to ensure their fundamental human rights are protected.

The scientific dimensions of homosexuality were no more conclusive than the theological ones. The committee made a humbling observation, confessing, "We had hoped that scientific facts could settle our debates, once and for all.... Our expectations were to be disappointed." The committee encountered divergent and nonconclusive scientific judgments on issues ranging from the definition of normal sexual behavior; the causal determinants of homosexuality; the feasibility of altering one's sexual orientation; and the advisability of encouraging such a change in one's sexual identity.

The committee did find scientific evidence that dispelled many fears and stereotypes surrounding homosexual lifestyles. Sexual orientation did not hinder one's parenting effectiveness, nor did it negatively affect one's proneness to abuse or violence. The study also concluded that many of the risky behaviors associated with gay men at the time of the study—namely having multiple sex partners and engaging in anal intercourse without adequate precautions—are unsafe and unhealthy practices for all people, whether homosexual or heterosexual.

Given the conflicting evidence, the Committee to Study Homosexuality did not reach a consensus. Ultimately, they listed four conclusions that a majority of the committee believed to be true:

- The seven biblical passages that specifically mention homosexual behavior "cannot be taken as definitive Christian teaching" because they represent ancient cultural practices, not enduring ethical declarations.
- Scientific evidence refutes the notion that homosexuality is a type of abnormal pathology, developmental flaw, or deviant behavior. Instead, it is a human variant with healthy and whole capacities.

- Emerging scholarly views in biblical, theological, and ethical studies affirm same-sex relationships that are "covenantal, committed, and monogamous."
- The above conclusions are further supported by the witness of God's grace in the lives of gay and lesbian Christians.

Based on these conclusions, the committee submitted a majority report that recommended to remove the incompatibility clause from the *Book of Discipline*. The majority report declared:

> The present state of knowledge and insight in the biblical, theological, ethical, biological, psychological, and sociological fields does not provide a satisfactory basis upon which the church can responsibly *maintain* the condemnation of all homosexual practice. (emphasis added)

However, the committee also included a minority statement that came to the opposite conclusion. Based on all the rational and scientific knowledge from all the same academic disciplines listed above, the minority report concluded that current scholarship:

> ...does not provide a satisfactory basis upon which the church can responsibly *alter* its previously held position that we do not condone the practice of homosexuality and consider this practice incompatible with Christian teaching. (emphasis added)

Despite the committee's best efforts, reasonable and rational deliberation did not resolve the division over homosexuality in the United Methodist Church.

Reaction

A few months before the 1992 General Conference, where the results of the study of homosexuality was to be presented for consideration and approval, controversy erupted. A group of 80 traditionalist clergy and laity gathered in Memphis and drafted a declaration of faith. Titled "The Memphis Declaration," the document listed several specific recommendations, including one that criticized the Report on the Study of Homosexuality. Perceiving the report as progressive overreach, the

Memphis Declaration called for the rejection of the report and further called for an end to any future denominational research on the topic. The declaration proclaimed, "The Biblical witness and the unbroken tradition of the Church provide the foundation of our understanding."[2] In the language of the Wesleyan Quadrilateral, the Memphis Declaration was pronouncing that Scripture and tradition had provided a clear verdict on the issue of homosexuality, and that reason could not alter it.

The report was a source of pointed debate during the 1992 General Conference. Ultimately, delegates did not formally approve the Report on the Study of Homosexuality. Instead, it was "received" but not "approved." The report, therefore, never became the official policy of the denomination. Delegates did, however, take several notable actions. Despite the report's unofficial standing, General Conference authorized it to be disseminated as a denominational resource. Furthermore, delegates approved the report's recommendation to add language to the *Book of Discipline* that supports the fundamental human rights and civil liberties of homosexual persons. Still, the ambitious goal of the committee to use rationality, logic, science, and reason to reach greater unanimity on homosexuality was never realized.

SHIFTING MEANING

A Contested Word

There are many challenges when attempting to have a rational discussion about homosexuality. Two underlying issues make it especially difficult for a reasonable dialogue even to begin. First, progressives and traditionalists disagree on how to define homosexuality. Second, even when the two factions can agree upon a basic definition of homosexuality, they will nevertheless dispute the implications of the term.

Many traditionalists and progressives find common ground in their dislike for the word "homosexual," yet they object to the word for different reasons. For traditionalists, the term implies an enduring and fixed personal trait. For this reason, they prefer "same-sex preference"

---

2 "The Memphis Declaration."

or "same-sex attraction" to emphasize the willful, volitional nature of homosexual behavior. Conversely, progressives criticize the term "homosexual" because it conjures up old images of clinical diagnoses of abnormal behavior. Furthermore, the word groups together a whole range of sexual identities into a single "other" category. For these reasons, progressives prefer to use specific terms like "lesbian" and "gay" to better describe a distinct identity. Also, the collective term LGBTQ is a reminder that this group is not a single identity, but actually a coalition of various sexual orientations that span across a spectrum: lesbian, gay, bisexual, transgender, queer, and more.

Origin of the Word "Homosexual"

Just as traditionalists and progressives disagree over the word "homosexual," they also dispute the significance of the origin of the word. The word "homosexual" (along with its parallel term, "heterosexual") was first coined in 1869 by Hungarian journalist-writer Karl-Maria Kertbeny. Initially published in the German language, the word was written in English for the first time in 1892. Its usage became increasingly common throughout the twentieth century.

The coining of the word "homosexual" is significant. Before then, there wasn't a word that described same-sex behavior as a stable, permanent aspect of a person's identity. Engaging in same-sex relations had always been perceived as an action that people did, but not as an integral expression of their inmost being. Kertbeny's new term contributed to people seeing homosexuality in this new way.

Progressive View. Progressives and traditionalists differ in the significance they attribute to the creation of the new term "homosexual." For progressives, it is a landmark moment that revealed a previously hidden dimension of human identity. It is a liberating moment when you have a label that captures something that you have experienced but cannot describe. How much more powerful is that moment when the new label reveals some trait or essence at the core of who you are? Furthermore, because there are no Hebrew or Greek words that connote this same meaning of enduring sexual orientation, the Bible's specific judgments toward same-sex acts seem less applicable. If there was no awareness that someone could inherently identify as a gay or lesbian person, it stands to reason that the Bible does not address the contemporary issue of homosexuality, at least not directly. In fact, to conceive of homosexuality as an inherent part of one's being makes it plausible to envision such an orientation as God-given and God-affirmed.

Traditionalist View. Traditionalists see the origination of "homosexual" very differently. For them, the fact that the word did not exist until the eighteenth century, and also that no similar sense of same-sex identity and orientation existed before then, casts doubts on the reality of such a concept. Traditionalist scholar Bill Arnold asserts that, rather than discovering an unknown dimension of human personality, the concept of homosexual orientation is a social construction. The term has been created in modern Western societies to label behavior that has existed throughout history, yet has never needed to be identified as a lifelong identity. Arnold states, "What we now call homosexuality is really only a behavior interpreted in different ways by different societies throughout history. It is not an inner essence that some people have and others do not." For this reason, he further recommends, "The idea of a fixed same sex orientation should be abandoned in the discussion. The concept of a homosexual inner essence, fixed at birth, won't hold up under close scrutiny."[3]

Psychiatry's Evolving Assessment

Beyond arguments over homosexuality's essentialist or constructed character, progressives and traditionalists also dispute the way psychiatrists and psychologists have conceptualized and diagnosed homosexuality over the years.

For much of the history of psychology and psychiatry, homosexuality has been diagnosed as a pathology. When the American Psychiatric Association published its first Diagnostic and Statistical Manual of Mental Disorders (DSM-I) in 1952, homosexuality was officially classified as a mental disorder and labeled as a "sociopathic personality disturbance." The DSM-II, published in 1968, softened the diagnosis somewhat, listing homosexuality as a form of sexual deviation. It was still a mental disorder, but it was no longer considered psychopathic. As advocacy for gay rights became prominent in the 1970s, activists challenged the professional

---

3 Bill Arnold, *Seeing Black and White in a Gray World,* 168-171.

society's position on homosexuality. A professional task force listened to the concerns of activists and evaluated the most recent research that found no difference between homosexuals and heterosexuals in their level of social functioning. As a result, the DSM-III of 1973 removed homosexuality from its list of mental illnesses, instead classifying it as a normal variation on the broad range of human sexual activity.

The decision to normalize homosexuality was not without controversy. Dissenters called for a referendum which allowed the entire American Psychiatry Association membership to vote on the matter. The decision to remove homosexuality from the DSM-III, thereby declassifying it as a mental disorder, was supported by 58% of all members. Additionally, the organization approved a formal statement that supported the civil rights of homosexual persons.

For progressives, the changing classification of homosexuality over time signifies a triumph of reason and rationality. By applying scientific methods in an effort to understand the experiences of LGBTQ people better, scientific research provides increasingly complete and accurate knowledge. Our capacity to apply reason to questions about homosexuality helps us eradicate ignorance, prejudice, and bigotry, including the biases stemming from our religious beliefs.

Traditionalists also value reason, yet they are often suspicious of the knowledge that has led to the normalization of same-sex behavior. They question the process by which these supposed scientific judgments were made. Traditionalists note the political pressure that was exerted upon the American Psychiatric Association during the process of publishing the DSM-III. Such incidents prompt traditionalists to wonder if much of the scientific knowledge being used to normalize same-sex behavior has less to do with objective inquiry and more to do with prevailing cultural values.

NATURE AND NURTURE

At the heart of the scientific debate over homosexuality is the question of its source. Is same-sex preference and orientation a matter of inherent genetics? Are childhood social experiences the reason people are LGBTQ? What about personal choice? Most progressive and traditionalist United Methodists agree that the issue is a complex one with multiple dimensions. However, the two factions differ in the degree to which they emphasize nature-based explanations and nurture-based ones. They further separate when considering the implications of these nature-nurture issues, especially regarding the question of the alterability of one's LGBTQ identity. Is changing one's sexual identity possible—and if so, is such a change desirable?

In this section, we focus on the rational arguments of three authors: one progressive (Dale Dunlap), one traditionalist (Howard Snyder), and one centrist (Adam Hamilton).[4]

A Complex Set of Causes

Progressive, traditionalist, and centrist United Methodists agree that a complex set of factors contribute to one's sexual identity, yet they frame the issue of nature and nurture in markedly different ways.

Progressive View. Progressives tend to place emphasis on innate, inherited factors as the chief cause of sexual orientation. Dale Dunlap notes that most theories cluster around psychological factors and genetic factors. While the evidence is still not conclusive, he suggests that genetic factors are becoming increasingly prominent as an explanation for homosexuality. Dunlap emphasizes that these innate causes shape everyone's sexual identity. "What is clear," he proclaims, "is that neither heterosexuality nor homosexuality is a deliberate, self-chosen orientation."

Traditionalist View. Howard Snyder reflects the traditionalist views when he is more hesitant about the role biology plays in the formation of one's homosexual preference. He declares, "No genetic basis for homosexuality has yet been established." Snyder goes on to say that the jury is still out and that a "number of people who have studied the matter see no credible evidence of a genetic basis for homosexual tendencies or behavior." Later, he acknowledges, "Certainly in some cases, genetic factors play a role in same-sex attraction and orientation." Snyder then quickly adds, "But no doubt in many cases—perhaps the majority—one's own life experiences play a key, and not always healthy, role."

---

4 The three primary sources for this section are: Howard Snyder, *Homosexuality and the Church*, 36-41; Adam Hamilton, *Confronting the Controversies*, 140-155; and Dale Dunlap, "Homosexuality and the Social Principles," in *Loyal Opposition*, 80-86. Though Dunlap's essay is rather dated, his arguments remain very consistent with the contemporary progressive perspective.

Centrist View. Adam Hamilton takes a middle-ground approach, suggesting not only are the causes of homosexuality complex, but different explanations may apply to different LGBTQ individuals. Some have their sexual orientation shaped *in utero*. Others develop a homosexual identity from their childhood environment, including childhood sexual trauma. Finally, Hamilton says some people choose to pursue homosexual relationships—either from failed opposite-sex relationships, an unfulfilled desire for companionship, or engaging in sinful activities like pornography and sexual experimentation. "In listening to the stories of homosexuals," writes Hamilton, "I believe there are likely multiple factors that might influence sexual orientation."

Moral Implications

Because progressives, traditionalists, and centrists reach different conclusions regarding the scientific scholarship on the causes of homosexuality, each group deduces markedly different moral implications from this body of knowledge.

Progressive View. Dale Dunlap's progressive position that homosexuality is based on naturally inherited genetic factors leads him to affirm the moral legitimacy of same-sex relationships:

> If one recognizes and affirms the reality of same-gender orientation as "natural" to that person's being—as I think we have no other option if we follow our theological guidelines faithfully—then to reject a "natural" expression of that orientation in a covenantal, responsible, faithful and loving relationship is fundamentally immoral.

Dunlap further asserts that if sexual orientation is not chosen, then it must be part of one's created nature. And if it is part of one's created nature, one's sexual orientation must be seen as a good, God-given gift. If we genuinely want to affirm, as the *Book of Discipline* instructs, that "sexuality is God's good gift to all persons," then we must encourage LGBTQ people to accept and embrace their sexual identity. As Dunlap puts it, "For gay persons, accepting their orientation is accepting the way God has created them, and thus, in the deepest sense, the way of accepting God."

Traditionalist View. Howard Snyder sees the issue much differently. Given his inconclusive posture toward the sources of same-sex desire, he contends that "social trends, cultural context, and particular experiences can lead heterosexual persons into homosexual behavior." After providing examples of straight, heterosexual individuals who had been tempted to act on same-sex opportunities, he speculates, "One wonders how many unsuspecting young men and women, boys and girls, are led into homosexuality who in other contexts would have grown into healthy heterosexual identities."

The above argument assumes that homosexuality is a voluntarily chosen option. However, Snyder also believes that same-sex intimacy is immoral even if science does firmly establish a genetic cause. "Even if a genetic basis were to be found," he writes, "that would not change the ethical question for Christians." Snyder compares homosexuality to alcoholism. Some people have a "particular susceptibility" to alcoholism, but a caring church does not endorse alcoholic behavior.

Similarly, if a firm genetic link is established for homosexuality, Christians should compassionately help those with same-sex proclivities, while avoiding support for the behavior. Snyder concludes, "Inborn tendencies, where they exist, do not justify indulging those tendencies in sinful or destructive ways. We seem clearly to understand this in other areas; there is no reason to make an exception in the case of homosexuality."

Centrist View. Because Adam Hamilton sees a variety of causes that account for whether or not people assume a homosexual identity, he likewise suggests a range of appropriate moral responses. Hamilton agrees with Snyder that some same-sex intimacy is the result of sinful behavior by heterosexuals who are misusing God's gift of sexuality. In such cases, Hamilton sides with the traditionalists and suggests that, just as we would help heterosexual people overcome other forms of sexual addictions and other dangerous sexual practices, we should teach people who misuse homosexual acts about the nature of sin and God's plan for sexual intimacy.

However, Hamilton is more conflicted about the moral implications for his two other categories of homosexual people, those who have been shaped either by their biology or their environment to identify as homosexual. "Here I find myself experiencing a high degree of ambiguity."

Hamilton continues that the typical responses of both progressives and traditionalists leave him dissatisfied, "yet I cannot clearly see a middle way." Hamilton cautiously suggests that perhaps homosexual relationships are not the "ideal" will of God, but such relationships can reflect God's "circumstantial" will in their lives if they embody the sacrificial, covenantal love expected in Christian marriage.

Can (and Should) Sexual Identity Change?

Alongside the moral implications of homosexuality, United Methodists have also grappled with the question of whether or not individuals can alter their sexual identity. Also, if the answer to this question is "yes," is such a change is advisable? We briefly explore these two questions by looking at the answers our traditionalist and progressive representatives offer.

Progressive View. Because they regard sexuality as something fixed exceptionally early in life, progressives are skeptical, even critical, of the prospect of changing one's LGBTQ orientation. Dunlap cites the American Psychological Association's official position that homosexuality is not an illness, as well as the association's opposition to portraying "Lesbian, Gay, and Bisexual people as mentally ill and in need of treatment due to their sexual orientation." Dunlap further notes the association's ethical concerns about any attempt to alter their clients' orientations, explicitly mentioning "reparative theory" as a suspect approach. Similarly, Dunlap notes that another APA, the American Psychiatric Association, "unanimously rejected therapy aimed solely at turning gays into heterosexuals." These professional psychiatrists cited concern that individuals subjected to such therapies could endure "depression, anxiety, and self-destructive behavior."

Traditionalist View. Snyder expresses hesitation about weighing in on the issue of homosexuals changing their sexual orientation. Ultimately, he offers some evidence that suggests one's sexual orientation can, indeed, change. He cites a 2007 study indicating that altering one's homosexual tendencies "may be possible" in some cases. Snyder quotes the study's claims that these new findings "appear to contradict the commonly held view of the mental health establishment that change of sexual orientation is highly likely to produce harm for those who make such an attempt." Beyond the study, Snyder also offers an anecdotal account of a college professor who renounced her lesbian identity and eventually marries a man.

Complementarity

When Christians speak of "complementarianism," they are often referring to a wide-ranging theory that involves every aspect of male-female relationships, including the division of gender roles and the exercise of marital authority. When United Methodists use the term, it is seldom applied so comprehensively. Instead, traditionalists within the denomination will use the word in a more limited biological sense, claiming that the harmonious, interconnected anatomy of male and female bodies is evidence of God's design for heterosexual intimacy. Below is a brief overview of the traditionalist and progressive positions on complementarianism as it applies to the debate over homosexuality.

Traditionalist View. Maxie Dunnam, former president of Asbury Theological Seminary, extols the many virtues and pleasures of sexuality, but he says that there is one virtue that is paramount: the perpetuation of humankind through the act of reproduction. Procreation is designed by God, and it can only be accomplished through the union of a man and woman. For Dunnam, then, "It is not unreasonable to say that since homosexual union cannot produce children, therefore it is 'unnatural,' both in the biblical and biological sense."[5] He continues, "The way God has created us makes sexual intercourse between male and female 'natural.' The female vagina is made to receive the male penis; the anus is not."

Dunnam connects this complementarian view with Scripture, including the proclamation from the Genesis account of creation and repeated by Jesus, that God created us male and female, and that the two shall become one flesh. For this reason, "the complementarity of male and female sexual organs provides a symbol at the physical level of the much deeper spiritual complementarity."

Progressive View. For the progressive, arguments from a complementarian view ring hollow for a couple of reasons. First, the church is not admonishing non-complementary sexual acts when heterosexuals engage in such behavior. There are no uproars or calls to prohibit sexual acts like cunnilingus, fellatio, or anal penetration between opposite-sex,

---

5   Quotes in this section are from Maxie Dunnam, "The Creation/Covenant Design for Marriage and Sexuality," in *Staying the Course*, eds. Maxie Dunnam and Newton Malony, 107-108.

heterosexual couples. Yet according to the traditionalist view, each of these behaviors involves the use of sex organs in ways for which they are not naturally designed.

Dale Dunlap, quoting David Matzko, suggests that the traditionalist view of complementarianism diminishes the profound depth of mutually-enriching relationships. True complementarity goes far beyond sexual acts, sexual organs, and sexual identity. Instead, a truly reciprocal relationship occurs when two people—of any sexual orientation—find one another and create a union that wholly completes each person. In Matzko's words, "I come to be who I am through the embodied presence of another." For Dunlap, this type of intense, mutual self-giving and self-discovery cultivates genuine complementarity, and it is not limited by one's sexual preferences.

CULTURAL CHANGES

For the remainder of the chapter, we shift away from analyzing homosexuality as a personal issue and now treat it as a social phenomenon. The United Methodist debate over homosexuality is not happening in a vacuum. Attitudes about LGBTQ issues are changing quickly in the United States and in much of the world. It is helpful to consider the sociological trends that are affecting these changing attitudes.

This section opens with a brief overview of the contemporary trend of legalizing same-sex marriage in modern societies, followed by an examination of the distinct differences between modern societies with postindustrial economies and more traditional nations that maintain agrarian cultures. Our exploration of cultural change concludes by summarizing the distinct ways progressives and traditionalists are responding to these trends.

Legalization of Same-Sex Marriage

In 2001, the Netherlands became the first country to recognize same-sex marriage. Anthropologists and historians have pointed to other eras in which isolated incidents and specialized rituals celebrated the relationship between two people of the same sex, but the action by the Netherlands was a genuinely historic milestone. Probably for the first time in human history (and surely for the first time in modern history), a nation legitimized the union of two people of the same sex. Homosexual marriage became the legal equivalent of heterosexual unions.

Other nations began to follow the Netherlands' lead. Belgium, Canada, Spain, South Africa, Norway, and Sweden all legalized same-sex marriage in the first decade of the twenty-first century.

In the United States, the legal parameters of marriage are typically a matter for the states to decide. In 2004, Massachusetts became the first state to legalize same-sex marriage. Additional states soon followed, and eventually 36 states legalized same-sex marriage over the next decade. Then, in 2015, the Supreme Court ruled that same-sex marriage would be legal in all 50 states.[6] Same-sex marriage was now the law of the land. Most Americans agree with the Supreme Court decision, as recent polls indicate that two-thirds of all adults approve of same-sex marriage.

In less than two decades, the world has gone from centuries without any consideration of same-sex marriage to now more than two-dozen countries that have legalized it. Why? What has changed to cause such a dramatic shift in the boundaries of marriage? To answer this question, we need to examine some other trends that have impacted our attitudes toward same-sex relationships.

From Traditional to Modern Society

For virtually all of human history, societies were structured around shared values and social obligations. The bonds of community were held together by a shared worldview that changed very little, so people's lives were typically very similar to the lives of their parents. Social change undoubtedly occurred, but for most of our ancestors, the pace of change was so slow that it was often imperceptible.

Approximately 200 years ago, this pattern changed. The Industrial Revolution brought a wave of social change that has transformed modern society. This transformation has paved the way for greater acceptance of LGBTQ people in multiple ways, namely the expansion of secularism,

---

6 Obergefell v. Hodges, 135 S. Ct. 2071, 2015.

pluralism, individualism and civil rights, as well as the redefinition of family. We briefly review each of these phenomena and consider how they have contributed to modern society's greater tolerance of homosexuality.[7]

Secularism. Modern society sees the world as something that can be understood and controlled. Increasingly, we turn to logic and science to answer our questions, and we are now less likely to trust sacred worldviews and religious explanations. The modern world has little respect for the traditional wisdom passed down through the ages, believing it has little to offer a world that operates so differently from the ancient world and continues to change at an increasingly rapid rate.

Not only do modern societies minimize the role of religion, but they also abandon the traditional values that usually accompany it. As religious belief and worship both decline in the United States and Western Europe, conventional values toward the family and sexual intimacy have also declined. Thus, the approval of homosexuality and same-sex marriage has increased. It's not a coincidence that, within the global United Methodist Church, opposition to homosexuality remains exceptionally high in Africa, where secularism has threatened traditional religious values much less than in the United States.

Pluralism. Alongside a secular worldview, modern societies also experience a great deal of pluralism. As populations grow and cities expand, people of varying races, ethnicities, and religions gather and interact with one another. When people are exposed to many other people with values notably different than their own, it becomes increasingly difficult for them to assume that their personal beliefs are uniquely true. Thus, people tend to develop a more relativistic worldview. With this relativistic worldview comes a greater acceptance and appreciation for diversity. Whereas traditional societies enforce strict gender expectations upon men and women, it is in modern pluralistic societies that the complexity and variety of lesbian, gay, bisexual, transgender, queer, asexual, and intersex identities are likely to be affirmed and welcomed by the larger society. Sexual identity becomes just one type of diversity among an array of many kinds of variety and difference.

---

7 This section summarizes several broad themes in the sociology of religion.

Individualism and Civil Rights. Traditional societies expect a significant degree of loyalty to one's family, faith, community, and country. The needs of the group are usually more important than the desires of the individual. In modern societies, however, individuals are encouraged to pursue their own dreams and to live their own lives. This doesn't mean that contemporary individuals avoid all commitments and obligations, but it does suggest that the depth of such loyalties does not compare to those in traditional societies. Under these conditions, individuals with LGBTQ orientations are more likely to feel empowered to pursue their distinctive identities and express their authentic selves.

With a heightened sense of individual autonomy, modern societies also place an increased emphasis on individual rights. Modern societies enact laws and take other measures to ensure that citizens are protected from unfair and discriminatory treatment. Over time, nations often expand individual rights to an increasingly broad swath of the population. Slavery is abolished. Women's suffrage becomes law. The Civil Rights Act is passed. New laws like the legalization of same-sex marriage are defended as another step in a long succession of expanding civil rights to ensure liberty and justice for all.

Redefining Family. In the ancient world, children were an essential part of the family. A source of economic productivity and security, bearing numerous children was necessary to offset the high rates of death that were a stark reality for all preindustrial societies. We see this value on procreation in the Bible, where God's first command to humankind is "Be fertile and multiply" (Genesis 1:28), and also when the Psalmist proclaims (Psalm 127:3, 5), "Children are a gift from the Lord.... The person who fills a quiver full with them is truly happy!" Conversely, infertility or "barrenness" is often depicted as a source of shame in ancient texts.

In modern societies, children are now an economic liability rather than an economic necessity. As a result, childbearing becomes less prominent. In the 200 years since the Industrial Revolution, fertility rates in the United States have plummeted from approximately seven children per woman to fewer than two. With the diminishing social obligation of childbearing, new family forms arise. The social stigma of childlessness has diminished significantly, and it is not uncommon for couples to choose not to have children. Just as significantly, marriage and family become less a matter of economic and social obligation and more a matter of personal choice and preference. The motivation for marriage shifts from social duty to personal fulfillment.

With these pronounced changes in the form and function of families in modern society, same-sex marriages become a viable alternative. There are no social consequences if gay and lesbian couples are not able to bear children. And if an individual is personally fulfilled from a same-sex union, then modern sensibilities affirm the individual's right to make such a choice. Of course, contemporary laws and medical technology make it possible for same-sex couples to raise and even bear children through means such as adoption, surrogacy, and artificial insemination. Some of these options, however, were not available even a few decades ago, and in many traditional societies around the world, they remain unattainable.

Reactions to Social Change

The traditionalist and progressive responses to these dramatic cultural shifts are evident in the labels we use for them. Traditionalists resist many of these social changes, preferring instead the traditional knowledge and the revered wisdom that has been passed down through the generations. Inversely, progressives prefer to adapt their beliefs and accommodate to the new realities of modern society, progressing to a more relevant religious perspective. Of course, traditionalists claim to embrace appropriate change and progressives argue that they have respect for worthy traditions, so one must not overgeneralize. Below is a brief summary of each group's response to the cultural changes above.

Progressive View. Progressives tend to see our rapidly changing world as a reality that we must accept and an opportunity we must embrace. The church has a responsibility to faithfully adapt its ministry to be a witness for Jesus Christ in an age that scarcely resembles the one in which he lived. Some of the changes we must decry, such as the casual treatment of sexuality that stems from individualism and secularism. But other changes we can embrace, such as the increasing affirmation of LGBTQ people and their right to express committed, sacrificial love in a union of marriage. For the progressive, changes like the latter are indicative of an expanding expression of God's love and justice in the world, which is cause for celebration.

In their recent book, *The Fight for Marriage*, Philip Cramer and William Harbison paint a bleak picture of Christianity's track record for civil rights. They note, "The Judeo-Christian tradition has an unfortunate and ugly history of using Scripture to support separation, slavery, and submissiveness of groups based on skin color, skin disease, ethnic origin, or gender." Elsewhere, they describe how church tradition was frequently used to oppose interracial marriage, comparing this form of discrimination to the more recent prohibitions against same-sex marriage. However, Cramer and Harbison are ultimately optimistic about the church because, over time, it expands its vision of equality and justice to an increasingly wider array of people. They declare, "During the past one hundred years, the church has, more often than not, been at the forefront of promoting equality, and most faith communities today fully embrace the sacred worth of all individuals."[8] The authors see a close parallel between the church's proclamation of equal justice for all and the growth of secular American civil law.

Traditionalist View. Traditionalists take a more cautious, and often more critical, stance toward the massive social changes of the past several decades. Their rational assessment of contemporary trends emphasizes the negative consequences of many of these changes. For example, traditionalist Bill Arnold argues that many of the supposed advances on behalf of LGBTQ people in modern society have troubling ramifications when viewed in a broader social context. He sees the affirmation of same-sex relationships as part of an overall trend that "destigmatized and demystified" all forms of non-marital sexuality, a trend which Arnold says creates an "anything goes" mentality so long as the sexual intimacy is between consenting adults. Such a cavalier attitude toward sexual activity ignores its consequences—consequences that have affected all people, but have been especially devastating for children and lower-income women. The supposed liberty that results from abandoning religious traditions in favor of the secular values of the sexual revolution is no liberty at all, says Arnold. Instead, "The heritage of that revolution has been enslavement."[9]

---

8 Philip Cramer and William Harbison, *The Fight for Marriage,* 11.

9 Bill Arnold, *Seeing Black and White in a Gray World,* 172-177. For this argument, Arnold draws heavily upon Mary Eberstadt's book, *Adam and Eve After the Pill: Paradoxes in the Sexual Revolution* (San Francisco, CA: Ignatius Press, 2012).

Arnold also represents the traditionalist view when he questions the comparison between today's struggle for LGBTQ rights and the civil rights that were gained by African Americans in the 1960s. He believes that the difference between the two movements is so profound "as to render the comparison irrelevant." United Methodists have always stood firmly in favor of protecting the civil rights for all people, but we must not assume that the protection of civil rights should result in the abandonment of ethics. Arnold insists, "The church must be allowed to fight for human and civil rights for all, while also calling us *all* to the highest standards of sexuality as discerned by Scripture, reason, tradition, and experience" (emphasis in original).

CONCLUSION: THE LIMITS OF REASON

What has this chapter taught us about applying reason to the issue of homosexuality? At the most basic level, it has shown us that reason and rationality do not inevitably lead to agreement. Even if we can concur on the data before us, our interpretation of the facts can diverge wildly. It is worth recalling the disheartening words from the 1992 Committee to Study Homosexuality: "We had hoped that scientific facts could settle our debates, once and for all.... Our expectations were to be disappointed."

Such a conclusion instills within us a sense of humility. The Apostle Paul reminds us of the limits of human knowledge in his first letter to the Corinthians (13:12), "For now we see only a reflection as in a mirror." Earlier in the same letter (8:1, NIV), he reminds us that our primary responsibility as disciples of Jesus Christ is not learning, but love: "We all possess knowledge. But knowledge puffs up while love builds up." Reason is a helpful tool as we discern the truth of God's creation in all its awe and splendor, but we should never be so confident of our mental capacities that we arrogantly assume we have attained complete and accurate knowledge.

While modesty about our intellectual capacities can be a healthy thing, Christians must also be wary of erring in the opposite direction. We must never distrust rationality and reason to the point of being anti-intellectual. Our ability to think and discern are God-given gifts that can and should be used to inform our Christian witness. As the *Book of Discipline* attests (¶105), "By our quest for reasoned understandings of Christian faith we seek to grasp, express, and live out the gospel in a way that will commend itself to thoughtful persons who are seeking to know and follow God's ways."

Although thoughtful Christians disagree over the morality of homosexuality, the application of reason has led to improved understanding. Our intellectual pursuits have taught us that human sexuality is a complex and multidimensional phenomenon. Simple dichotomies such as "straight" and "gay" fail to capture the diverse ways people experience their sexual desires. We have also learned that the causes of homosexuality are just as complex. Only a few decades ago, same-sex behavior was either dismissed as a mere personal choice or overly simplified to a single cause such as a dominating mother or a distant father. Now, because of thoughtful analysis, traditionalists and progressives alike agree that sexual identity is grounded in a multifaceted set of physiological, psychological, and environmental factors.

Despite these points of agreements, deep divisions remain over the ethical inferences drawn from our knowledge of homosexuality. Rational inquiry has not provided a consensus on the moral implications of same-sex behavior. Progressives and traditionalists continue to differ on fundamental issues. We may agree that sexual preference is deeply embedded in one's sense of self, but is changing one's same-sex identity either feasible or desirable? We may concur that the human rights of LGBTQ people should be protected, but does this extend to the right of marriage? Both sides provide rationales for their answers to these questions, yet neither side has been able to convince the other.

QUESTIONS TO CONSIDER

Consider the following questions. If you are discussing in a group, commit to a respectful dialogue in which the goal is hearing and understanding one another rather than winning and advancing a particular point of view.

1. The United Methodist *Book of Discipline* states that "all truth is from God." It continues that it is good for us to make connections between "revelation and reason, faith and science, grace and nature." In what ways do you find science and religion compatible? Are there also ways that you see them in tension with one another? Does the relationship between faith and reason affect your understanding of homosexuality in any way?

2. Proposals to formally study homosexuality have encountered resistance, and the 1992 General Conference never approved the findings of the Committee to Study Homosexuality. Why do you think such studies have typically been met with skepticism and opposition?

3. What terminology are you most accustomed to using when discussing homosexuality? Have you given thought to why you prefer those terms? Which terms do you find objectionable, and why? (Refer to Appendix A for a list of terms.)

4. Before 1973, the American Psychiatry Association listed homosexuality as a mental disorder. Now, with most other professional scientific organizations, the association regards homosexuality as a normal variation of human sexuality. Do you agree with the American Psychiatry Association's current position? Why do you think their position shifted in 1973?

5. Do you view homosexuality more as a matter of nature or nurture? In other words, are you more likely to think of same-sex desire as something you're born with, something you learn, something you choose, or some combination of these? What are your reasons for this position? How does your understanding of nature and nurture influence your moral stance on homosexuality?

6. Do you support the Supreme Court's decision to legalize same-sex marriage? Why do you think the United States and other modern societies have legalized same-sex marriage at this moment in history? How should the United Methodist Church respond to this social change?

7. Which changes from traditional to modern societies do you think have had the most significant impact on the growing acceptance of homosexuality in the United States? How has society's changing views of marriage, family, and sexuality impacted the debate over LGBTQ issues?

8. Progressives tend to emphasize the similarities between the legalization of interracial marriage and the legalization of same-sex marriage, while traditionalists tend to highlight the differences. Which view do you find most convincing, and why?

Photo by Mike DuBose, United Methodist News Service. Used with permission.

Chapter 6

CONCLUSION: RESOLVING OUR DIVISIONS?

THE BROKEN CHALICE

The accompanying photo sits framed in my family room. The broken chalice is from the 2004 General Conference in Pittsburgh. On the day before the photo was taken, delegates had voted to uphold the United Methodist's traditional positions on homosexuality, maintaining that same-sex behavior was incompatible with Christian teaching. Shortly after the midday celebration of Holy Communion, LGBTQ supporters staged a protest on the conference floor to express their frustration over the denomination's unresponsiveness to their pleas. During that protest, a pastor lifted the chalice off of the altar and threw it to the ground, shattering it to pieces. The presiding bishop, with the help of others, gathered the pieces together. Someone reassembled the chalice as best they could and later placed it back on the altar as shown in the photo.

I was not at the 2004 General Conference. In fact, only recently did I learn of this memorable event. However, the broken chalice has become a powerful symbol to me, a vivid reminder of the brokenness of my beloved United Methodist Church. We are a divided and shattered Body of Christ, held together in the most precarious of ways.

I am certainly not the first to see the broken chalice as a potent symbol for the church. Shortly after General Conference, Jorge Acevedo, a prominent traditionalist pastor and a recent member of the Commission on a Way Forward, also equated the broken pieces of the chalice with the brokenness of the divided church. Acevedo described the event as "sacramental desecration." Suggesting that such an action would never be tolerated at a local church, Acevedo lamented, "Our bishops said and did nothing. Our General Conference said and did nothing. I said and did nothing, and I am sorry." He concludes his thoughts by exclaiming, "Shame on us!"[1]

Julie Todd, an ordained elder and leader in the progressive Love Prevails movement, interprets the events differently than Acevedo. "There was no chaos, no storming the altar, no desecration of the sacrament," says Todd of the unplanned chalice smashing. Rather, "there was a holy anger that took shape in a prophetic act. A movement of the Spirit interceded to express anguished sighs too deep for words." Todd continues, "In the breaking of the cup, Christ spoke to the real brokenness of the moment." She also declares that the violent act toward the chalice symbolically expressed the violence that has been experienced by LGBTQ people and their allies. She writes, "There was a need for a deep and spiritual release of the violence that had just been done to the queer body of Christ. Because when votes are cast against the very existence of LGBTQ lives, that is what happens: violence. Christ's body crucified again. To not act in the face of such violence does further violence."[2]

Yet again, we see the deep, deep division within the United Methodist Church. Was the iconic smashing of the communion chalice a sacrilegious moment or a sacred one? Was it disgraceful or divine? One single act, but two markedly contrasting interpretations. We are, indeed, a deeply divided denomination.

Sadly, our divisions have only grown deeper and wider. The United Methodist Church is on the brink of schism. It is not an overstatement to say that the fate of the denomination will be determined at the specially called General Conference in St. Louis on February 23-26, 2019.

This chapter provides an overview of the current status of our denomination.[3] The first half presents the significant events that have

---

1 Jorge Acevedo, "Sacramental Desecration at General Conference 2004."

2 Julie Todd, "On the Body Being Broken."

3 Unless otherwise noted, the details in this chapter come from official news sources of the United Methodist Church.

occurred from the 2016 General Conference through September 2018, the time of this book's printing. The second half will focus on looking ahead to the 2019 special General Conference. Most importantly, it will provide a detailed summary of all three plans that have been proposed by the Commission on a Way Forward, with a quick look at a few additional proposals from others. The goal of this chapter is to provide a balanced and thorough overview so readers will be adequately informed as United Methodists embark on this perilous moment in their history.

The subject matter of this chapter requires extensive references to various features of the United Methodist organizational structure. Readers who are not familiar with the local, regional, national, and international connectional configuration of the denomination may benefit from consulting Appendix C.

THE 2016 GENERAL CONFERENCE

The atmosphere surrounding LGBTQ issues at the General Conference of May 2016 in Portland was especially tense. A year prior, the United States Supreme Court made the historic ruling that same-sex marriage was now legal for the entire country, giving progressives hope that similar change could happen within the United Methodist Church. At the same time, the traditionalist influence on the denomination had grown even stronger, given the expanding influence of both Africa and the southernmost jurisdictions in the United States. The tension had also intensified two years prior, when prominent traditionalist leaders made a public appeal to separate from the denomination, and rumors circulated that these leaders were going to make a formal proposal of schism in 2016. During the General Conference, tension mounted even further as progressives protested the church's lack of inclusiveness by tying themselves together and singing "Blest be the Tie that Binds." One hundred clergypersons came out and publicly avowed their LGBTQ identity.

It was in this environment that Bishop Bruce Ough, President of the Council of Bishops, addressed the General Council with a call for unity. During that address, he reminded the delegates that bishops are not voting members at General Conference. The chief responsibility of bishops is to preside, implying that it was up to the delegates to determine a way forward.

Several delegates were frustrated by Bishop Ough's remarks, believing that it demonstrated a lack of leadership that left the denomination stuck in a "painful condition." Pastor Tom Berlin addressed his fellow delegates, stating, "Bishop Ough said that at General Conference, the role of the bishop was to preside. Quite frankly, Bishop, we think it's your role to lead. We are asking for your leadership." Other delegates also pleaded for the bishops to intervene and assist in finding a way out of the impasse between traditionalists and progressives over LGBTQ issues. Unprecedented in United Methodist history, delegates passed a motion that asked the bishops to intervene in General Conference. The motion directed the bishops to recommend to the General Conference a plan of action, a way to move forward.

The following day, Bishop Ough presented a proposed way forward for the embattled denomination. The bishops recommended that General Conference refrain from any further legislative debates concerning homosexuality, instead taking time to "pause for prayer." The bishops asked the delegates for the authority to name a special commission that would thoroughly analyze the denomination's positions on human sexuality and to make recommendations on revisions to the *Book of Discipline* if needed. This proposed commission would reflect the geographical and theological diversity of the church.

Although traditionalists were skeptical that such a commission was necessary, the body narrowly approved the Council of Bishops' proposed plan by a vote of 428-405. The action was historic. Not only was it the first time that General Conference had asked the bishops to intervene in their legislative affairs, but it was also only the second time that the Council of Bishops called a special session of General Conference. The only other time had been nearly 50 years earlier when a special session was set for 1970. Even then, that conference was not intended to resolve a crisis. Instead, it was a necessary gathering to finish extensive legislative details in the wake of the merger that created the United Methodist Church two years prior. The special session of 2019 will be the first time the denomination has called an emergency gathering because of a crisis that threatens its future.

Later in 2016, the Council of Bishops formally created the 32-person Commission on a Way Forward. The commission included eight bishops, 11 elders, two deacons, and 11 lay members. Nine countries were represented. The commission had at least three openly gay members and two prominent traditionalist leaders. The bishops also set the date of the special General Conference for February 23-26, 2019, in St. Louis.

AFTERMATH OF GENERAL CONFERENCE

About two months after the 2016 General Conference, Bishop Ough reported on a meeting to finalize plans for the Commission on a Way Forward. However, he opened his report by noting the "profound dissonance" between what General Conference had agreed to in May—pausing for prayer—and the flurry of exacerbating actions that occurred in the ensuing weeks. He then added, "The landscape has changed dramatically." Bishop Ough cited three events that spurred the change:

1. the declarations of several regional annual conferences that they will not comply with the LGBTQ prohibitions in the *Book of Discipline;*
2. the election of Karen Oliveto, an openly lesbian clergyperson, as bishop in the Western Jurisdiction; and
3. the impending gathering of a new traditionalist organization, the Wesleyan Covenant Association.

Ough lamented that these actions have "opened deep wounds and fissures within The United Methodist Church and fanned fears of schism."[4] Below, we examine each of these critical developments and their impact on the current state of the United Methodist Church. We conclude with one additional issue that surfaced after the bishop's letter, namely the confusion over the proper scope of the 2019 special session of General Conference.

---

4 Bruce Ough, "The Commission on a Way Forward."

Declarations of Non-Compliance

Shortly after the 2016 General Conference, regional annual conferences convened to attend to local matters. Of the 56 annual conferences in the United States, approximately a dozen took some type of formal action to defy or decry the LGBTQ restrictions in the *Book of Discipline*. Each of the annual conferences in the Western Jurisdiction made some official declaration, as did the northernmost annual conferences in the Northeastern Jurisdiction and a couple of annual conferences in the North Central Jurisdiction. For example, the California-Pacific Conference approved a policy stating that they would not use sexual orientation as a criterion for ordination. Similarly, both the California-Pacific Conference and the Desert Southwest Conference voted to refrain from taking any judicial action against anyone who may be charged with violating the *Book of Discipline*'s restrictions related to homosexuality. The Oregon-Idaho Conference issued a statement that supported the "gifts and graces" of LGBTQ people in ordained ministry.

On the East Coast, the New England Conference supported a resolution declaring that it "will not conform or comply" with the sexuality restrictions in the *Book of Discipline*. The New York Annual Conference went beyond proclamations and acted, ordaining (or commissioning for ordination) four people who had openly declared themselves as LGBTQ individuals.

Some annual conferences responded in a more traditionalist manner. In response to the many declarations of non-compliance in other annual conferences, the South Georgia Conference passed a motion requesting that their bishop refuse to receive or appoint any clergy member who has publicly declared an intent to disregard the current language of the *Book of Discipline* regarding sexuality. The Baltimore-Washington Conference, typically viewed as a progressive region, did not approve the ordination of Tara "T.C." Morrow, a married lesbian who was seeking to become an ordained deacon.

Election of Karen Oliveto

As progressive annual conferences proclaimed their opposition to the *Book of Discipline*'s bans on same-sex behavior, the Western Jurisdiction undoubtedly caused the greatest uproar when it elected Karen Oliveto to serve as a bishop in their jurisdiction. Oliveto, who had served as pastor of San Francisco's famously progressive Glide Memorial Church, became the first openly LGBTQ person to serve alongside other bishops in the highest position of the United Methodist Church. She was appointed to serve as bishop of the Mountain Sky Area, a region encompassing churches in Colorado, Montana, Utah, Wyoming, and a small portion of Idaho.

The reaction to Oliveto's election was predictably pronounced and divided. While progressives hailed the election as a historic milestone for LGBTQ inclusion, prominent traditionalist pastor Rob Renfroe decried, "If the Western Jurisdiction wanted to push the church to the brink of schism, they could not have found a more certain way of doing so."

Bishop Bruce Ough, speaking on behalf of the Council of Bishops, issued a formal statement confessing that "we find ourselves in a place where we have never been." Ough outlined the murkiness of the situation: As a clergyperson in good standing, Oliveto was certainly eligible to be elected as bishop by her jurisdiction. At the same time, being a self-avowed practicing homosexual is a chargeable offense, and bishops are subject to the same moral standards as all ministers. Ough clarified that the Council of Bishops has no constitutional authority to intervene in the legislative activities of United Methodist regional conferences and jurisdictions, but that the council was carefully monitoring the situation.

Shortly after Oliveto's election as a bishop, the South Central Jurisdiction petitioned the Judicial Council (the highest court in the United Methodist Church) to determine whether or not her consecration as bishop violated church law. The Judicial Council subsequently ruled that the actions of Western Jurisdiction did, indeed, violate church law. However, the Judicial Council also ruled that Bishop Oliveto "remains in good standing" until the completion of a formal review process. Bishop Ough once again spoke on behalf of the Council of Bishops, noting that the decision did not alter any standards in the *Book of Discipline* because only General Conference has the authority to do that. Still, he empathized, "We acknowledge that the decision [by Judicial Council] does not help to ease the disagreements, impatience and anxiety that permeates The United Methodist Church over the matter of human sexuality, and particularly this case. Our compassion and prayers of intercession extend to all those who are hurt, relieved, confused or fearful."

To date, no further action has been taken, and Bishop Oliveto continues to lead and serve the annual conferences within the Mountain Sky Area.

Launching the Wesleyan Covenant Association

Progressives were not alone in rousing controversy in the wake of the 2016 General Conference. In October of that year, 1,800 traditionalists gathered in Chicago to unveil the Wesleyan Covenant Association. As described on their website, the organization is a network of "Spirit-filled, orthodox churches, clergy, and laity who hold to Wesleyan theology." The fledgling organization associates with other traditionalist renewal organizations like the Confessing Movement, Good News, and United Methodist Action.

The Wesleyan Covenant Association emphasizes three commitments: (1) the authority of Scripture and the Lordship of Jesus Christ; (2) a unified response to the recommendations of the Commission on a Way Forward; and (3) developing a plan for a "positive and faithful" future. The new organization presents a unified voice that advocates for retaining the current policies and standards for same-sex behavior in the denomination, warning that any decision to relax these principles will be unacceptable to their members.

Many United Methodists perceive that the Wesleyan Covenant Association is preparing to break from the United Methodist Church to form their own traditionalist denomination. Such a schism has already occurred in three other mainline Protestant denominations, each having experienced cultural conflict very similar to that in the United Methodist Church. The Episcopal Church, the Presbyterian Church (USA), and the Evangelical Lutheran Church of America have each had a portion of their church splinter to form new traditionalist denominations (respectively, the Anglican Church of North America, the Evangelical Covenant Organization of Presbyterians, and the North American Lutheran Church). To many, the Wesleyan Covenant Association seems poised to take the same action.

Initially, leaders of the Wesleyan Covenant Association minimized schism as an option and emphasized how all members had been loyal to the church in every way. Still, many of the association's founders were also at the forefront of calling for an "amicable separation" in 2014 (see

Chapter 3). Over time, talk of separation has become more prominent. In their self-description on their webpage, the Wesleyan Covenant Association notes that change is coming to the United Methodist Church, and they commit themselves to "working on plans for a revitalized twenty-first-century Methodism that can be implemented either within a United Methodist structure or outside it."

Many traditionalists argue that it is the progressives, not the Wesleyan Covenant Association, who are fanning the flames of schism. They contend that it is progressives who are vocally ignoring denominational standards of human sexuality, and that it is progressives who are openly defying administrative and judicial procedures of the denomination. Thus, it is the progressives who have already in effect separated themselves from the faithful membership of the United Methodist Church.

Confusion Over General Conference Scope

The critical motion passed by the 2016 General Conference stated that bishops would appoint a commission "to do a complete examination and possible revision of every paragraph of the *Book of Discipline* concerning human sexuality and explore options that help to maintain and strengthen the unity of the church." It further stated that the bishops would call a special General Conference exclusively devoted to resolving the denomination's impasse on this issue. Exact details of the process were not thoroughly spelled out, but the Council of Bishops committed "to maintain an on-going dialogue with this Commission as they do their work, including clear objectives and outcomes."

Despite these good intentions, confusion ensued in early 2018 over what the General Conference had actually approved. The Council of Bishops presumed that the Commission on a Way Forward would report to the bishops, and then the bishops would submit a specific report with recommendations to the special General Conference to consider in 2019. Some experts contended that the Council of Bishops was overstepping its supervisory and administrative role in the church and transgressing into legislative affairs, which are the specific purview of General Council only.[5] The matter was presented to the Judicial Council, and in May

5 William Lawrence and Sally Curtis AsKew, "Constitutional Methodism in Crisis: Historical and Operational Perspectives on Divisions Threatening United Methodism," in *Methodist Review.*

2018 Judicial Council ruled that any proposed legislation for the 2019 special General Conference must be submitted by the Commission on a Way Forward, not the Council of Bishops. The court stated, "There is nothing in the proceedings of the 2016 General Conference suggesting that the Commission on a Way Forward was supposed to submit its recommendations to the Council of Bishops."

The Judicial Council further ruled that legislative proposals at the special General Conference are not limited to those recommended by the commission. Other United Methodist individuals and groups may also submit petitions to the special General Conference "as long as the business proposed ... is in harmony with the purpose stated in the call." The court did not specify what constitutes being "in harmony" with the called purpose of the special General Conference, instead leaving that matter for the delegates to determine.

All petitions, including those submitted by the Commission on a Way Forward, were required to be submitted no later than July 8, 2018. The Judicial Council will then rule on the constitutionality of each of these proposals in October. Delegates of the special General Conference will deliberate over all of the valid petitions on February 23-26, 2019, in St. Louis.

THREE PROPOSED PLANS

The final report of the Commission on a Way Forward includes three plans for the special General Conference to consider: (1) the One Church Plan, (2) the Connectional Conference Plan, and (3) the Traditionalist Plan.

- *The One Church Plan* keeps the United Methodist Church unified as a single denomination, hence the name. The church would take no formal position regarding LGBTQ issues like same-sex marriage, so clergy and congregations would have a great deal of latitude to follow their own consciences and to effectively minister according to their local context. Many progressives approve this plan, though some do so reluctantly. This plan was endorsed by a majority of members of the Commission on a Way Forward. Of the 32 members serving on the Commission, 18 of them support this plan (several members supported more than one plan). Also, the One Church Plan is the only one endorsed by the Council of Bishops.

- *The Connectional Conference Plan* dissolves the five regional jurisdictions in the United States and in their place creates three values-based "connectional conferences": traditionalist, centrist/ unity, and progressive. Annual conferences, congregations, and clergy would each have the opportunity to select the connectional conference to which they would like to belong. Each connectional conference would have its own distinctive approach to ministry, yet each would still remain connected to the other connectional conferences through shared essential doctrines and certain joint ministries and agencies. This is often viewed as a centrist plan that allows a level of unity amidst diversity, but it faces significant administrative hurdles. Of the 32 members serving on the Commission on a Way Forward, 12 of them support this plan (several members supported more than one plan).

- *The Traditionalist Plan* retains the United Methodist Church mostly in its current form, including the incompatibility clause, the prohibitions on same-sex marriage, and the restrictions on ordaining self-avowed practicing homosexuals. It also adds greater levels of accountability to ensure adherence to church doctrines and policies, especially as it relates to homosexual behavior. The plan offers a way for those who can't abide by the traditionalist stance on human sexuality to exit the denomination yet still maintain an institutional relationship with the United Methodist Church. As the name indicates, this is the preferred plan for many traditionalists. Of the 32 members serving on the Commission on a Way Forward, nine of them support this plan (several members supported more than one plan).

Below is an overview of each plan, including concerns and criticisms that each has received. The complete plans are detailed and nuanced. The focus here will be specifically on how each of these plans affects matters related to homosexuality. Furthermore, the emphasis of these summaries will be how each plan may impact local congregations and clergy in the United States, with a secondary focus on the repercussions for annual conferences, jurisdictions, and international regions. Other important topics are beyond the scope of this book, including clergy pension issues; the impact on United Methodist agencies; the logistics of transitioning to a new organizational structure; and the specific wording that would be used in the revisions to the *Book of Discipline*. Readers who would like to know these additional details are encouraged to access the final report of the Commission on a Way Forward, which is available on the United Methodist website.[6]

Within these parameters, each of the summaries below abbreviates, reorders, and paraphrases the key points offered by final report of the Commission on a Way Forward. Often, these overviews rely on the exact phrasing of the commission's final report.[7] After describing the plans presented by the commission, this section concludes with a few additional proposals that have been petitioned by others: the progressive Simple Plan, the traditionalist Exit Path, and the traditionalist Plan of Dissolution.

The One Church Plan

Overview. The goal of the One Church Plan is to maintain the connectional nature of the United Methodist Church. The structure of the denomination remains intact, ministering to the world as a single, unified church. At the same time, churches and pastors are given a great deal of flexibility so they can minister effectively in their particular social context. The Commission on a Way Forward report characterizes this combination of a unified church with enhanced latitude as a "generous unity."

To achieve the type of flexibility that the One Church Plan seeks, several critical changes would be made that impact the church's position on homosexuality. Foremost, it removes from the *Book of Discipline* the statement that homosexual behavior is incompatible with Christian teaching. It likewise erases the current language that restricts pastors and churches from conducting same-sex weddings. Thus, pastors who so desire would be permitted to perform same-sex weddings, and congregations that so desired could hold LGBTQ weddings in their sanctuaries.

---

6 http://www.umc.org/who-we-are/way-forward-report-released-in-all-four-official-languages-of-general-confe

7 "Commission on a Way Forward's Report to the General Conference."

At the same time, the One Church Plan adds language to the *Discipline* that intentionally protects the religious freedom of pastors and churches who choose not to perform or host same-sex weddings. No congregations or pastors are compelled to act contrary to their convictions. Those who wish to officiate and host same-sex marriages may do so, and those who do not want to do so may refrain.

Like marriages and weddings, the One Church Plan also removes language from the *Discipline* that explicitly prohibits annual conferences from ordaining self-avowed practicing homosexual persons. Instead, each annual conference is permitted to establish its own ordination policies. This means that one annual conference may have ordination standards that allow LGBTQ people to be ordained, but a neighboring annual conference prohibits self-avowed practicing homosexuals from ordination. Lesbian and gay candidates who are in annual conferences that elect not to ordain LGBTQ people may opt to transfer to annual conferences that do.

This flexibility and freedom of conscience extends to higher levels of church administration as well. The One Church Plan adds language to the *Discipline* that protects the ethical convictions of bishops, who would be protected from ordaining self-avowed practicing homosexual persons if their conscience does not permit. Likewise, boards of ordained ministry (the committees that represent annual conferences to discern the qualifications of candidates seeking ordination) would have the option of creating guidelines that opt not to ordain self-avowed practicing homosexual persons.

Globally, the One Church Plan has no impact on those conferences outside the U.S. where same-sex marriage, or even homosexual behavior itself, is illegal. For such international regions, it is permissible to retain the current language of the *Book of Discipline*. In other words, global regions would be allowed to form specific policies regarding homosexual behavior suitable to their local culture.

In effect, under the One Church Plan, the United Methodist Church becomes neutral and noncommittal regarding the morality of same-sex relationships, allowing every region and every clergy member to minister according to one's personal conscience and their local context. Proponents of the plan say that this gives churches the flexibility and space they need to maximize the presence of a United Methodist witness in as many places in the world as possible. The plan affirms that we can minister with a unity of mission, even if we don't have a unity of practice.

The One Church Plan also signifies that our current impasse over marriage and ordination of homosexual persons does not rise to the level of a church-dividing issue. Such division, some may argue, is not in keeping with the will of God for a community of believers who share a common heritage, doctrine, beliefs, and ministry.

Concerns and Criticisms. Below is a brief summary of the major objections to the One Church Plan:

1. Most traditionalists oppose the plan because it compromises the church's historic opposition to same-sex behavior. Traditionalist organizations like the Wesleyan Covenant Association have unequivocally stated that they cannot support a plan that effectively makes acceptance of LGBTQ marriage and ordination the default position of the church.

2. Many progressives will likely support this plan, but they are not without their objections. Specifically, progressives object that the One Church Plan still allows discrimination toward LGBTQ people. Clergy, congregations, and annual conferences are all allowed to restrict the ministry of lesbian and gay people if they so choose.

3. Despite the plan's name, some worry that the One Church Plan creates an inconsistent, divided church in which there would be no consistent policy from church to church, region to region. People, both inside and outside the denomination, will not know what type of United Methodist Church they are attending (though some argue this is already the case).

4. Allowing United Methodist leadership (bishops and boards of ministry) to act on their personal conscience creates the potential for very convoluted and inconsistent systems of ordination.

5. Several people fear that this plan will foment significant divisions at the local church level, as many congregations will be required to debate their policies regarding same-sex weddings in their sanctuaries.

6. Some people worry that this plan erodes the distinctive connectional model of church organization, reflecting more of a congregational model where local churches become more autonomous and less interwoven with the rest of the denomination.

The Connectional Conference Plan

Overview. The Connectional Conference Plan creates three distinct branches within the United Methodist Church while retaining a unified core of shared doctrines and ministries. This plan disbands the five regional jurisdictions in the United States and replaces them with three values-based "connectional conferences." Each of these connectional conferences would have its own distinctive definitions of accountability and justice. In other words, the distinctiveness of these branches would not be based on their regional location, but rather their theological perspective. Thus, there would likely be one traditional, one progressive, and one centrist ("unity") connectional conference.

Each connectional conference would have its own policies regarding LGBTQ weddings and ordination. One likely scenario is that the traditional conference would maintain the denomination's current prohibitions, while the progressive branch would expect all pastors to support LGBTQ weddings and ordination. The centrist-unity conference would take no official position on homosexuality and allow pastors and congregations each individually to decide, much like the proposed One Church Plan.

These branches are called "connectional" conferences because, although each would have certain distinct policies, they would still be integrated with one another in cooperative relationships in mission and ministry. The conferences would share an abbreviated General Conference that would focus mostly on worship and the sharing of ministry ideas. Similarly, there would be a shortened "General" *Book of Discipline* that all three conferences would hold in common. Each branch, however, would also have its own General Conference and extended *Book of Discipline*, each reflecting the distinct policies and convictions of the branch. Many of the current boards, agencies, and ministries of the United Methodist Church would continue to be shared, but it would also be possible for connectional conferences to selectively opt out of their support of certain ones.

The Council of Bishops would include the bishops from all three branches, serving mostly as a collegial learning and nurturing body. Each connectional conference would have its own "College of Bishops," which would exercise authority over their particular conference. Judicial Council would operate much the same way: a denomination-wide Judicial Council encompassing all three connectional conferences, and then separate "judicial courts" for each branch.

Sorting the church into the three conferences would occur through a cascading process. First, the five regional jurisdictions would vote on which connectional conference they desire to join. Second, each of the local annual conferences within a jurisdiction would have the option of voting to move to a different connectional conference if it is dissatisfied with the choice made by their jurisdiction. Third, each congregation within an annual conference will have the opportunity to move to a different connectional conference if they are discontent with the decision made by their annual conference. At each level, voting takes place only if there is dissatisfaction with the choice made by the administrative level above.

Each United Methodist pastor would join the connectional conference of her or his choice. Pastors may choose to affiliate with more than one conference.

Globally, each international region (called "central conferences") would have the choice of becoming their own distinct connectional conference with the same powers as the three connectional conferences in the United States. Alternatively, international regions could join one of the three connectional conferences in the states.

Concerns and Criticisms. Below is a brief summary of the major objections to the Connectional Conference Plan:

1. The plan is a sweeping restructuring of the denomination. Such widespread changes require amendments to the United Methodist Constitution, which must be passed by a two-thirds majority of delegates at the special General Conference. This will be a very challenging feat.
2. The plan involves a significant number of overlapping ministries and administrative responsibilities.

3. Many observers fear that the sorting process will create prolonged debates that will cause animosity at every administrative level of the denomination. The result could potentially harm morale and membership.

4. Traditionalists may still be discontent that they are affiliated with a denomination that allows one of its branches to marry and ordain LGBTQ people. Conversely, progressives may still be discontent that they are affiliated with a denomination that permits a branch to prohibit LGBTQ people from getting married and being ordained.

5. It's not clear where one's primary religious identity will lie—the United Methodist Church as a whole or the connectional conference to which they belong.

6. Some fear that separating into values-based conferences is just a prolonged intermediary step that will eventually and inevitably lead to schism.

The Traditionalist Plan

Overview. The Traditionalist Plan[8] maintains the current stance of the church regarding the definition of marriage and its teaching on human sexuality. It advocates one unified moral position on the issues of marriage and sexuality for the entire denomination.

This plan continues to affirm all current United Methodist policies regarding homosexuality. LGBTQ persons are welcome to attend worship services, participate in church programs, receive the sacraments, be baptized, and join as members. However, the Traditionalist Plan

---

8 The Traditionalist Plan has some atypical features in the final report of the Commission on a Way Forward. There are actually two versions of the Traditionalist Plan included in the report, each less thoroughly developed than the One Church and Connectional Conference plans. In November 2017, upon presenting sketches of all three plans to the Council of Bishops, the bishops instructed the council to further develop only the One Church Plan and Connectional Conference Plan. Then, in May 2018, just days before the commission's final meeting, the bishops instructed the commission to also include the Traditionalist Plan in their final report. Lacking time to develop the third plan fully, the commission included only their original sketch from months before. However, a few bishops also submitted their own version of the Traditionalist Plan to the commission, and their version was included as an appendix of the commission's final report. The summary in this book attempts to integrate the central themes of the two versions of the Traditionalist Plan.

also maintains all of the current prohibitions on LGBTQ marriages and ordination. In fact, this plan would broaden the current definition of "self-avowed practicing homosexual" to include persons living in a same-sex marriage or civil union, or persons who in any way publicly state that they are practicing homosexuals.

At the heart of the Traditionalist Plan is a requirement to uphold, enforce, and maintain the *Book of Discipline*'s present standards on marriage and ordination. This requirement applies to every pastor, bishop, congregation, and annual conference. Formal measures of accountability will require that each of these bodies affirm and certify their fidelity to the denomination's ethical standards of human sexuality.

The Traditionalist Plan acknowledges the sincere and conscientious objections some people have to the church's current stance and practices regarding homosexuality. The plan calls for a "gracious and respectful" way for those who cannot live within the current bounds of church law to leave the United Methodist Church. Those who choose to leave are able to form their own denomination and "institute practices in keeping with their understanding of Scripture, tradition, reason, and experience." Such a newly formed denomination would be autonomous, but it could also maintain a close affiliation with The United Methodist Church through a "concordat agreement" as described in the *Book of Discipline* (¶574). The Methodist Church of Puerto Rico is an example of a denomination that was formerly part of the United Methodist Church, then separated to become autonomous, but nevertheless chose to maintain a close relationship through a concordat agreement.

In the Traditionalist Plan, annual conferences would be given time to affirm and certify their support for the denomination's moral standards of human sexuality. Those annual conferences that do not certify within the allotted time period would be encouraged to form an autonomous, affiliated, or concordat church. In other words, they would be asked to leave the United Methodist Church.

Under this plan, local churches do not need to vote on anything unless they disagree with their annual conference's choice to either remain in or depart from the denomination. Accordingly, local congregations that disagree with their annual conference's decision to leave the denomination could vote to stay with the United Methodist Church. The opposite is also true: Local churches that disagree with their annual conference's decision to remain in the United Methodist Church could vote to withdraw from the denomination and unite with the new autonomous, affiliated, or concordat denomination that will presumably form.

Identical to the process for congregations, clergy members who could not maintain the *Discipline's* standards that prohibit LGBTQ marriage and ordination would also be expected to leave, presumably to minister in the new autonomous, affiliated, or concordat denomination. Any United Methodist clergy who breach the church's standards of human sexuality would be subject to repercussions. Clergy would be required to surrender their credentials if they were found guilty of breaking provisions related to same-sex marriage in the *Book of Discipline.*

The Traditionalist Plan would only minimally impact the activities and ministries of United Methodist agencies and boards. Similarly, the global impact of the Traditionalist Plan would presumably be negligible, as most of the international regions (known as central conferences) would likely support the continuation of traditionalist standards of human sexuality.

Concerns and Criticisms. Below is a brief summary of the major objections to the Traditionalist Plan:

1. The plan maintains the status quo on standards of human sexuality, which has been a major source of the denomination's current division.

2. The plan essentially banishes progressives from the denomination, striking some people as harsh and exclusionary.

3. The plan has a strong focus on restrictions and punishments, which seems contrary to the denomination's emphasis on grace. Also, the proposed measures of accountability may not be constitutional.

4. Traditionalists have long made the argument that the crisis in the church is not about homosexuality per se, but about deeper theological issues. However, the Traditionalist Plan provides little theological or scriptural foundation. All of the grounds for removal from the denomination focus on matters of human sexuality.

5. Some people have expressed concern that this plan was not thoroughly vetted by the Commission on a Way Forward. The 2016 General Conference approved a precise procedure to

develop proposals for the special General Conference of 2019, and the Traditionalist Plan does not appear to have followed this procedure (see the previous footnote).

Additional Plans and Proposals

In addition to the three plans submitted by the Commission on a Way Forward, there are several additional plans submitted by others for consideration at General Conference. While most observers don't expect these other proposals to gain widespread acceptance, there are three that warrant a brief overview. Progressives have recommended the Simple Plan, while traditionalists have suggested the Exit Path and the Plan of Dissolution.

The Simple Plan. The United Methodist Queer Clergy Caucus has proposed legislation that has one underlying goal: "to remove the language from the *Book of Discipline* that excludes LGBTQ people from full participation in the church."[9] Based on a plan originally drafted by the Reconciling Ministries Network, the Simple Plan would remove same-sex behavior as a barrier to ordination. Similarly, same-sex marriages would be permissible, and pastors would participate in such ceremonies at their discretion as their conscience allows. Similar to the One Church Plan, no clergy members would be compelled to act against their consciences. Pastors who oppose same-sex marriage would have the freedom of conscience to decline such ceremonies. They would not be required to officiate same-sex ceremonies, nor would church sanctuaries be required to accommodate same-sex weddings.

Exit Path. Although the Wesleyan Covenant Association makes it clear on their website that the organization did not submit any formal petitions for the 2019 special General Conference, prominent traditionalist leaders such as their president did.[10] The Exit Path makes it possible for local churches to disaffiliate from the United Methodist Church if a super-majority of church members declare that they have "irreconcilable

---

9 "A Simple Plan," UM Queer Clergy Caucus.

10 The Wesleyan Covenant Association has posted both the Exit Path and the Plan of Dissolution on its website: https://wesleyancovenant.org/petitions/.

conflict for reasons of conscience" with the doctrines of the denomination or the requirements in the *Book of Discipline.*

Historically, congregations that disaffiliate from the United Methodist Church are not permitted to take any property with them, because all property is held in trust on behalf of the denomination. The Exit Path makes an exception during this tumultuous time, so local congregations can more easily break from the United Methodist Church if they are dissatisfied with the decisions or the direction of the denomination. While the Exit Path would apply to any local church, it has been traditionalist congregations that have been most vocal about the possibility of separating.

Plan of Dissolution. Keith Boyette, president of the Wesleyan Covenant Association, also submitted a Plan of Dissolution. The plan proposes that the differences within the United Methodist Church have become so irreconcilable that it is best to dissipate the denomination. Such dissolution would allow new denominational structures to emerge, "allowing the resulting entities to move forward in ministry as they are led by God." The presumption is that a minimum of two new Christian bodies would form—one traditionalist, one progressive, and perhaps one centrist. If this plan were to pass in 2019, the scheduled 2020 General Conference would be held for the sole purpose of dissolving the United Methodist Church. The plan further encourages such steps to be taken "with the utmost of Christ-like grace, charity, and generosity toward one another."

THE 2019 SPECIAL GENERAL CONFERENCE

At the time this book was published (September 2018), organizers were still finalizing details for the special General Conference of the United Methodist Church. Below is some basic information on this historic event.

The special session of General Conference will be held February 23-26, 2019, in St. Louis, Missouri. The venue will be The Dome at America's Center Convention Complex.

The special General Conference of 2019 will be comprised of 864 delegates. As with all General Conferences, half of the delegates will be clergy and the other half will be laity. Approximately 58 percent will be from the United States, and 30 percent will hail from Africa. The remaining delegates will represent the Philippines, Europe, and Eurasia, with a small number of delegates representing "concordat" denominations that share a formal association with the United Methodist Church.

The vast majority of delegates at the 2019 special General Conference will be the same representatives from 2016. A couple of annual conferences, however, have opted to elect new delegates to ensure that LGBTQ voices participate in this momentous decision.

The estimated expense of the special General Conference totals slightly more than $3.7 million. Initially, there was a $700,000 shortfall in the conference budget, and organizers planned to charge a $200 registration fee for non-delegates who wanted to attend. After widespread objection, that idea was withdrawn. There will be no charge for those who wish to observe the special General Conference.

The exact agenda has not been set at the time this book was published, but General Conference will surely include separate times of worship and legislative action. Regarding the latter, because this is a specially called General Conference, delegates will be limited to considering matters related to the specific charge given to them. Thus, all deliberation will focus on the denomination's standards and policies concerning human sexuality in the *Book of Discipline* and exploring options to strengthen the unity of the church. Such deliberations will likely include debate over the three plans presented in the final report of the Commission on a Way Forward, as well as other proposals submitted by other individuals and groups.

All proposals submitted prior to General Conference must ultimately be declared constitutionally sound by the Judicial Council. The council will make these rulings in October 2018. However, delegates may also introduce new recommendations from the floor of General Conference, and Judicial Council may also be asked to rule on the constitutionality of any legislation that passes.

Most proposed legislation will require a simple majority vote to pass, and the actions of General Conference would be binding for the whole denomination, provided the actions are deemed constitutional by Judicial Council. However, some of the proposed changes (particularly in the Connectional Conference Plan) would require changes to the Constitution of The United Methodist Church. Such changes require a two-thirds affirmative vote by the delegates. Then, if passed by General Conference, the constitutional legislation would be sent to all the regional annual conferences. Two-thirds of all the aggregate members from all the annual conferences would be required to approve the change before it would be enacted into church law.

CONCLUSION: A PRECARIOUS FUTURE

The United Methodist Church is a remarkable denomination with noble intentions. Not only is the mission of the church admirable—to make disciples of Jesus Christ for the transformation of the world—but the way in which our denomination pursues that mission is also commendable. At its foundation, the United Methodist connectional system strives to put our faith into action by applying democratic ideals. General Conference, the only body that can make and change official church policies and standards, is comprised of as many as 1,000 duly elected Christians to represent the full spectrum of our international denomination. Equally represented by clergy and laity, we gather from different races, ethnicities, nationalities, and ideologies to proclaim Jesus Christ as Lord and to seek how best to live as His Body.

These worthy aspirations are being put to the test. The breadth of our denomination's diversity is being stretched to its limits. We live in a world of rapid social change, and Christians must decide how to respond to such change. Do we resist it? Do we embrace it? Do our choices enhance or diminish our pursuit to lovingly embody the good news of Jesus? When it comes to the church's response to homosexuality, we are not responding to these questions with one voice. Our diverse denomination is answering these questions in manifold ways, and there is little indication that a more unified response is on the horizon.

As the largest mainline Protestant denomination in the United States, the United Methodist Church is not alone in this crisis. As noted earlier, each of the next three largest mainline traditions—Lutheran, Presbyterian, and Episcopalian—have experienced remarkably similar divisions between traditionalists and progressives, and each has experienced schism over the issue of homosexuality in recent years. The United Methodist General

Conference in February, 2019, will surely determine whether or not our denomination will experience the same fate.

This has been a difficult book to write. The story is not a happy one. The fissures from our frustrations and mistrust run deep. Undoubtedly, these wounds will leave scars. At the time of this book's publication, one is hard-pressed to find any optimism regarding a way forward that does not involve more sorrow and pain. Throughout all my research for this book, the only time I recall encountering the word "joy" was a remark by the General Conference business manager, who was enthused by the favorable hotel rates one can get in St. Louis in February.

But the end of the story has not yet been written. We will have a much better idea of how the story ends—or at least how it proceeds—in February 2019. The decisions that our denomination makes in the coming months will have far-reaching implications for the witness of the church in the United States and across the world. And yet, as significant as this moment is, our divisions and decisions concerning homosexuality are only a tiny part of a much larger, much grander story, a story that spans before the start of human history, and indeed, unfolds beyond the reach of space and time. In the bleakest of circumstances, our faith reminds us to turn our eyes upon Jesus and to place our trust in the Triune God who creates us, redeems us, sustains us, and transforms us. As a people called United Methodist, we can take comfort from John Wesley's dying words, "Best of all, God is with us."

QUESTIONS TO CONSIDER

Consider the following questions. If you are discussing in a group, commit to a respectful dialogue in which the goal is hearing and understanding one another rather than winning and advancing a particular point of view.

1. This chapter begins with a story of a broken chalice that became a powerful symbol to the author. Do you have a seminal experience, event, or symbol that has become profoundly important to you concerning the church and homosexuality?

2. What is your opinion of the 2016 General Conference's unprecedented request for the Council of Bishops to intervene by establishing a commission and a special General Conference to address our impasse over homosexuality? Do you think this was the best way forward? If not, what actions do you think should have been taken?

3. Do you think it is constructive for progressive annual conferences to openly defy the standards for human sexuality specified in the *Book of Discipline*? Why or why not?

4. Do you think it is constructive for traditionalists to form an organization (the Wesleyan Covenant Association) in which the leaders have advocated an amicable separation between traditionalists and progressives? Why or why not?

5. What features of the One Church Plan do you find the most appealing? Which features concern you?

6. What features of the Connectional Conference Plan do you find the most appealing? Which features concern you?

7. What features of the Traditionalist Plan do you find the most appealing? Which features concern you?

8. Are there other plans beyond the three presented by the Commission on a Way Forward that appeal to you? If so, which alternative plan do you like, and why?

9. What are your hopes and aspirations for the 2019 special General Conference? Given the current crisis in the United Methodist Church, what would be the most favorable outcome for you? How might such a result be achieved?

Appendix A:
GLOSSARY OF HUMAN
SEXUALITY TERMS

Below is a list of terms used by the United Methodist Commission on a Way Forward in its deliberations, as reported in their publication "Finding a Way Forward: Resources for Witness, Contextual Leadership, and Unity." With a few exceptions, their glossary was adapted from terms used by the Human Rights Campaign, the nation's largest LGBTQ civil rights organization. The commission added a few clarifying remarks, which are included below with their original emphasis. The terms denoted with an asterisk (*) were not used by the commission, but are included in this glossary because of their use in this book.

Ally: A person who is not LGBTQ but shows support for LGBTQ people and promotes equality in a variety of ways.

Androgynous: Identifying and/or presenting as neither distinguishably masculine nor feminine.

Asexual: The lack of a sexual attraction or desire for other people.

Bisexual: A person emotionally, romantically or sexually attracted to more than one sex, gender or gender identity though not necessarily simultaneously, in the same way or to the same degree.

Cisgender: A term used to describe a person whose gender identity aligns with those typically associated with the sex assigned to them at birth.

Closeted: Describes an LGBTQ person who has not disclosed their sexual orientation or gender identity.

Coming out: The process in which a person first acknowledges, accepts and appreciates their sexual orientation or gender identity and begins to share that with others.

Gay: A person who is emotionally, romantically or sexually attracted to members of the same gender.

Gender identity: One's innermost concept of self as male, female, a blend of both or neither—how individuals perceive themselves and what they call themselves. One's gender identity can be the same or different from their sex assigned at birth.

*Homosexuality: A term to describe a sexual orientation or behavior in which a person feels physically and emotionally attracted to people of the same sex. Traditionalists often dislike the term because it suggests a fixed identity, while progressives often dislike it because of its historical usage as a clinical term to pathologize gay and lesbian people.

Intersex: "Intersex" is a general term used for a variety of conditions in which a person is born with a reproductive or sexual anatomy that doesn't seem to fit the typical definitions of female or male.

Lesbian: A woman who is emotionally, romantically or sexually attracted to other women.

LGBTQ: An acronym for "lesbian, gay, bisexual, transgender and queer." *The acronym is sometimes lengthened to LGBTQIA. This includes persons who identify as intersex and asexual.*

Living openly: A state in which LGBTQ people are comfortably out about their sexual orientation or gender identity—where and when it feels appropriate to them.

Outing: Exposing someone's lesbian, gay, bisexual or transgender identity to others without their permission. Outing someone can have serious repercussions on employment, economic stability, personal safety or religious or family situations.

Queer: A term people often use to express fluid identities and orientations. Often used interchangeably with "LGBTQ." *Queer has been used as a hurtful slur, but it has been reclaimed and adopted as a positive description of one's identity. In some cultural contexts, the word "queer" is not associated with sexual orientation or gender identity at all. Rather it is synonymous with "odd," "peculiar," or "not quite right." Sometimes it can even mean "questionable" or "suspicious."*

Questioning: A term used to describe people who are in the process of exploring their sexual orientation or gender identity.

*Same-sex attraction: A term that is used to describe the experience of feeling emotionally and/or sexually attracted to people of the same sex. Religious traditionalists often use this term to differentiate between attraction and behavior, and also to avoid terminology that implies a fixed homosexual orientation.

Sexual orientation: An inherent or immutable enduring emotional, romantic or sexual attraction to other people.

Transgender: An umbrella term for people whose gender identity and/or expression is different from cultural expectations based on the sex they were assigned at birth. Being transgender does not imply any specific sexual orientation. Therefore, transgender people may identify as straight, gay, lesbian, bisexual, etc.

Appendix B:
SOCIAL PRINCIPLES:
HUMAN SEXUALITY

Statements relevant to the debate over human sexuality occur in several locations throughout the United Methodist *Book of Discipline*. Below is the most comprehensive statement of human sexuality, found in "The Nurturing Community" section of the *Discipline*'s Social Principles.

¶161 G: Human Sexuality

We affirm that sexuality is God's good gift to all persons. We call everyone to responsible stewardship of this sacred gift.

Although all persons are sexual beings whether or not they are married, sexual relations are affirmed only with the covenant of monogamous, heterosexual marriage.

We deplore all forms of the commercialization, abuse, and exploitation of sex. We call for strict global enforcement of laws prohibiting the sexual exploitation of children and for adequate protection, guidance, and counseling for abused children. All persons, regardless of age, gender, marital status, or sexual orientation, are entitled to have their human and civil rights ensured and to be protected against violence. The Church should support the family in providing age-appropriate education regarding sexuality to children, youth, and adults.

We affirm that all persons are individuals of sacred worth, created in the image of God. All persons need the ministry of the Church in their struggles for human fulfillment, as well as the spiritual and emotional care of a fellowship that enables reconciling relationships with God, with others, and with self. The United Methodist Church does not condone the practice of homosexuality and considers this practice incompatible with Christian teaching. We affirm that God's grace is available to all. We will seek to live together in Christian community, welcoming, forgiving, and loving one another, as Christ has loved and accepted us. We implore families and churches not to reject or condemn lesbian and gay members and friends. We commit ourselves to be in ministry for and with all persons. (See Judicial Council Decision 702)

From *The Book of Discipline of The United Methodist Church—2016*. Copyright © 2016 by The United Methodist Publishing House. All rights reserved. Used by permission.

Appendix C:
UNITED METHODIST
ORGANIZATION

The United Methodist Church is organized as a connectional denomination. This means that every local United Methodist congregation is interconnected with all the others through an extensive network of formal relationships. The denomination practices a representative democracy form of governance. Although there are important differences, there are also helpful similarities between the organizational structure of the United Methodist Church and the governmental structure of the United States of America. Using this comparison, we describe the essential features of the structure of the United Methodist Church.

These descriptions are adaptations from the "Who We Are" section of the United Methodist website: http://www.umc.org/who-we-are. The comparisons to United States governance are added.

General Conference (similar to the U.S. House of Representatives)

The United Methodist General Conference is similar to the legislative branch of the U.S. government. More precisely, it has many comparable features with the U.S. House of Representatives. General Conference is comprised of several hundred delegates (never more than 1,000) who represent the international distribution of United Methodists. Like the U.S. House of Representatives, the delegates of General Conference are proportionally distributed according to the size of the membership within the various regions of the United Methodist Church.

General Conference is the only entity in United Methodism that can set church policy and officially speak for the denomination. Unlike the U.S. House of Representatives, no individual can veto legislation passed by General Conference, though the Judicial Council (see below) can determine the constitutionality of any action adopted by General Conference.

The General Conference of the United Methodist Church is a single representative body. However, within this one legislative body are two types of delegates, clergy and laity, of which there is always an equal number. Delegates deliberate and vote on petitions and resolutions that have been formally proposed by a broad and diverse array of sources from within the denomination.

Since 1968, General Conference has met every four years. Each four-year cycle is called a quadrennium. The most recent General Conference was in 2016 in Portland, Oregon. On rare occasions, special General Conferences may be called to address critical matters. The special 2019 General Conference is only the second special session ever called in United Methodist history, and it is the first such session called to address a denominational crisis.

The *Book of Discipline* (similar to the U.S. Constitution, the U.S. Legal Code, and more)

The *Book of Discipline* is a multi-purpose collection of essential documents of the United Methodist Church. It includes the church's constitution, theological statements, social principles, official policies, and administrative order. Every four years, delegates at General Conference vote to amend various statements and policies of the *Discipline*. Thus, the *Book of Discipline* is the resource that encompasses all the binding decisions of each General Conference.

Judicial Council (similar to the U.S. Supreme Court)

The Judicial Council is the highest judicial body of the United Methodist Church. It is comprised of nine members, each elected by the General Conference. The Judicial Council determines the constitutionality of legislation passed by either General Conference or smaller regional conferences (see below). Judicial Council further determines whether or not specific actions of official church bodies conform to the policies and standards in the *Book of Discipline*, and they also hear appeals of decisions made by lower judicial bodies.

Council of Bishops (similar to the executive branch of government)

The United Methodist Church does not have a president, a pope, or an archbishop. It does, however, have a type of executive branch of church governance that oversees the order, administration, and spiritual life of the church. This is the responsibility of the Council of Bishops. There are 66 active United Methodist bishops, 46 from the United States and 20 from international regions. Once elected, bishops are assigned to serve and oversee a specific geographic area. These areas typically include one or more annual conferences (see below). In this way, each bishop bears some similarity to governors in the United States, who each lead and serve a particular state.

The authority of the bishops is both spiritual and practical. As individuals, they are the moral and administrative leaders of their respective regions. Collectively, they form the Council of Bishops, which is charged with providing oversight and spiritual direction for the church.

Although bishops have moral and administrative authority, they do not have any legislative powers. They do not vote at General Conference, they may not veto legislation. In fact, bishops may not personally address General Conference unless they are presiding over the conference's proceedings or the delegates have granted them special permission to speak.

Jurisdictions and Central Conferences (no similarity to U.S. government)

The United Methodist Church is divided into broad areas. In the United States, these areas are called jurisdictions, and there are five of them: Northeastern, Southeastern, North Central, South Central, and Western. A map of these jurisdictions is below.

Internationally, the comparable regions are called central conferences. There are seven central conferences: three in Africa (Africa, Congo, and West Africa); three in Europe (Central and Southern Europe, Germany, and Northern Europe and Eurasia); and one in the Philippines.

Jurisdictions and central conferences provide training events and other ministry resources for the smaller regions called annual conferences (see below). Like the international General Conference, jurisdictional conferences meet every four years. It is here where bishops are elected and assigned to annual conferences within the jurisdiction.

Annual Conferences (similar to U.S. states)

Each jurisdiction and central conference consists of smaller regional units called annual conferences. Annual conferences play a central administrative role within the United Methodist Church.

There are 54 annual conferences in the United States. These are roughly the size of states, but the boundaries of annual conferences are often different from those of states. The following map outlines each annual conference. There are 75 international annual conferences outside of the United States.

"Annual conference" can be a confusing term in the United Methodist Church because it actually has three meanings. In addition to being a regional body, annual conference is also an organizational unit, consisting of the presiding bishop and staff, that oversees the region's spiritual and administrative needs. Finally, "annual conference" is also the name for the yearly meeting that is held by each annual conference to address church matters pertaining to its region.

Like General Conference, annual conferences always have an equal number of lay and clergy delegates. Unlike General Conference, annual conferences meet annually.

Districts (similar to U.S. counties)

Each annual conference is divided into smaller units called districts. Each district is headed by a district superintendent, an ordained elder who has been appointed by the bishop for a six-year term. The district superintendent (often called the "DS") supervises and supports the ministries of local churches and pastors within the district.

Local Churches

The local church is the fundamental unit of the denomination. It is the place where United Methodists gather to worship, fellowship, and prepare to engage and serve their communities and world. The worship, service, and outreach of local churches are part of a larger global connection of ministries that comprise the United Methodist Church. Every local church is connected to a district. Churches and their pastors are supported by and accountable to the District Superintendent.

JURISDICTIONS AND ANNUAL CONFERENCES
OF THE UNITED METHODIST CHURCH

WESTERN JURISDICTION   NORTH CENTRAL JURISDICTION   NORTHEASTERN JURISDICTION

SOUTH CENTRAL JURISDICTION   SOUTHEASTERN JURISDICTION

Appendix D:

RECOMMENDATIONS
FOR GROUP DISCUSSION

In the months leading up to the special General Conference in February 2019, and likely also for a long while afterward, many United Methodist congregations will have group conversations about our denominational divisions over homosexuality. *United Methodists Divided* is written to be a helpful resource for such discussions. Below are three different sets of recommendations for holding constructive group discussions: the author's personal recommendations, recent denominational resources for leading "courageous conversations," and an older set of denominational recommendations for holding civil deliberations. These recommendations can be useful for any group discussions, even if this book is not used.

Author's Recommendations

Below are some recommendations for group discussion on sensitive topics by the book's author, Dale McConkey. These recommendations are based on over 25 years of teaching college students, as well as his years leading discussions on theological issues as a college chaplain, a local pastor, and a Wesley Foundation director.

- ***Adapt to your context.*** Different contexts will call for different types of discussion. As a facilitator, you will be in the best position to anticipate the dynamics of your group. Thoughtful reflection on how your particular group may respond to the sensitive issues at hand will be more valuable than any list of general recommendations.
- ***Encourage participants to read beforehand.*** Make clear the expectations for everyone in the group to read the assigned portion of the book before the discussion. The explicit purpose of *United Methodists Divided* is to show that both traditionalists and progressives have thoughtful reasons for believing the way they

do. If group members don't read the book before gathering, they will be unaware of the various positions, and the discussion will rely on uninformed opinions.

- ***Establish the goals, tone, and structure.*** Perhaps most important to a successful discussion on difficult topics is knowing what you hope to accomplish. As famed *Seven Habits* author Stephen Covey says, "Begin with the end in mind." Before any discussion begins, clearly establish the intended goals of the group, the tone in which the goals will be pursued, and the anticipated format the discussion will take. For example, one admirable goal might be to seek understanding and learning, not debating and convincing. Similarly, an admirable tone would be respectful and civil, not combative or judgmental.

- ***Know your group.*** Will it be difficult to get your group to talk, or will it be difficult to keep them quiet? Will they be passionate and insistent about their opinions, or will they be more inquisitive and curious? Anticipating the dynamics of the conversation will help maximize its fruitfulness.

- ***Assign a moderator/facilitator.*** For each session, strongly consider assigning a moderator who is charged with keeping the group focused on the agreed-upon goals using the agreed-upon tone. For some groups, it will be preferable to have the same moderator for every gathering. For others, it may make sense to rotate the responsibility.

- ***Keep comments brief and to the point.*** Prevent a single voice from dominating the discussion. Be sure everyone has a chance to share so that a diversity of perspectives can be heard.

- ***Avoid overgeneralizations and totalizing comments.*** Statements like "progressives don't believe in the Bible" or "traditionalists hate LGBTQ people" lead to stereotypes and rarely help advance understanding and learning. Encourage subtlety and nuance.

- ***Adapt the discussion questions for your use.*** The discussion questions at the end of each chapter are meant to be prompts, not a specific agenda.

Courageous Conversations

Discipleship Ministries, an agency of the United Methodist Church, has created a "toolbox" of resources to help local churches engage in important but difficult conversations. The Courageous Conversations website has many excellent materials, including two discussion outlines that are particularly relevant to group discussions about homosexuality:

> An outline for a discussion about "Human Sexuality" can be found at:
> *https://www.umcdiscipleship.org/resources/courageous-conversations-about-human-sexuality*
>
> An outline for a discussion about "A Way Forward" can be found at:
> *https://www.umcdiscipleship.org/resources/courageous-conversation-about-the-way-forward*
>
> General information about the Courageous Conversations initiative can be found at:
> *https://www.umcdiscipleship.org/topics/courageous-conversations*

Guidelines for Civility

In 1997-1998, the United Methodist General Council on Ministries sponsored a Commission on Christian Unity and Interreligious Concerns. The commission had an equal number of religious traditionalists and progressives, and the commission's goal was to find ways to help the church become more unified. From their deliberations, the commission developed a list of "Guidelines for Civility in The United Methodist Church." These are the ten guidelines:

1. Respect the personhood of others, while engaging their ideas.
2. Carefully represent the views of those with whom we are in disagreement.
3. Be careful in defining terms, avoiding needless use of inflammatory words.
4. Be careful in the use of generalizations; where appropriate offer specific evidence.

5. Seek to understand the experiences out of which others have arrived at their views. Hear the stories of others, as we share our own.
6. Exercise care that expressions of personal offense at the differing opinion of others not be used as means of inhibiting dialogue.
7. Be a patient listener before formulating responses.
8. Be open to change in your own position and patient with the process of change in the thinking and behavior of others.
9. Make use of facilitators and mediators where communication can be served by it.
10. Always remember that people are defined, ultimately, by their relationship with God—not by the flaws we discover or think we discover in their views and actions.

BIBLIOGRAPHY

Acevedo, Jorge. "Sacramental Desecration at General Conference 2004." *The Florida Conference of the United Methodist Church.* May 21, 2004. https://www.flumc.org/newsdetail/926933.

Adams, Christopher. "Sharing in Faith: A View from Both Sides." *The People of the United Methodist Church.* June 5, 2015. http://www.umc.org/what-we-believe/sharing-in-faith-a-view-from-both-sides.

Alexander, Kate. "United Methodists on Edge of Schism Over Homosexuality." *Baltimore Sun,* February 3, 2001. http://articles.baltimoresun.com/2001-02-03/news/0102030179_1_united-methodist -church-homosexuality-church-law/2.

Arnold, Bill. *Seeing Black and White in a Gray World: The Need for Theological Reasoning in the Church's Debate Over Sexuality.* Franklin, TN: Seedbed Publishing, 2014.

The Book of Discipline of the United Methodist Church. Nashville, TN: The United Methodist Publishing House, 2016.

Boswell, John. *Same-Sex Unions in Premodern Europe.* New York, NY: Villard Books, 1994.

Calvin, John. *Calvin's Commentaries, Volume XIX.* Grand Rapids, MI: Baker Publishing House, 1979.

Carter, Ken. "'God Hath Bid All Humankind': Generous Orthodoxy and our Mission with Gays and Lesbians in the United Methodist Church." *The Florida Conference of the United Methodist Church.* July 25, 2013. https://www.flumc.org/blogdetail/653465.

Chesterton, G.K. *Orthodoxy.* New York, NY: John Lane Company, 1908.

The Church Studies Homosexuality. Nashville, TN: Cokesbury, 1994.

Collins, Kenneth J. "Human Sexuality and the Unity of the Church: Toward a Faithful United Methodist Witness." n.d. https://www.gbhem.org/sites/default/files/08collins_human_sexuality_and_the_ unity_of_the_church.pdf.

"Commission on a Way Forward's Report to The General Conference." n.d. http://s3.amazonaws.com/Website_Properties/council-of-bishops/news_and_ statements/documents/Way_Forward_Report_-_Final_-_ENGLISH.pdf.

Cooperman, Alan. "Case of Gay Worshiper in Va. Splits Methodists." *Washington Post,* October 28, 2005. http://www.washingtonpost.com/wp-dyn/content/article/2005/10/27/ AR2005102702148.html.

Cooperman, Alan. "Gay Minister to Face Jury of Methodist Peers." *Washington Post,* November 29, 2004.
http://www.washingtonpost.com/wp-dyn/articles/A18635-2004Nov28.html.

Cooperman, Alan. "Lesbian Minister Defrocked by United Methodist Church." *Washington Post,* November 1, 2005.
http://www.washingtonpost.com/wp-dyn/content/article/2005/10/31/AR2005103100971.html?noredirect=on.

Cramer, Phillip F. and William L. Harbison. *The Fight for Marriage: Church Conflicts and Courtroom Contests.* Nashville, TN: Abingdon Press, 2018.

Dunlap, E. Dale. "Homosexuality and the Social Principles." In *The Loyal Opposition,* edited by Tex Sample and Amy E. DeLong, 71-87. Nashville, TN: Abingdon Press, 2000.

Dunnam, Maxie D. "The Creation/Covenant Design for Marriage and Sexuality." In *Staying the Course,* edited by Maxie D. Dunnam and H. Newton Malony, 104-114. Nashville, TN: Abingdon Press, 2003.

Fenton, Walter B. "Invoking the Holy Spirit." *Good News Magazine,* April 11, 2017. https://goodnewsmag.org/2017/04/invoking-the-holy-spirit/.

Fenton, Walter B. "No Consequences for Talbert's Defiance." *Good News Magazine,* January 6, 2015.
https://goodnewsmag.org/2015/01/no-consequences-for-talberts-defiance/.

Furnish, Victor Paul. "The Loyal Opposition and Scripture." In *The Loyal Opposition,* edited by Tex Sample and Amy E. DeLong, 33-42. Nashville, TN: Abingdon Press, 2000.

Gangler, Daniel R. "Creech Found Guilty." *Affirmation.* November 18, 1999. http://www.umaffirm.org/cornews/creech59.html.

Hahn, Heather and Sam Hodges. "GC2016 Puts Hold on Sexuality Debate." *United Methodist News,* May 18, 2016.
http://www.umc.org/news-and-media/bishops-ask-for-hold-on-sexuality-debate.

Hamilton, Adam. *Confronting the Controversies: Biblical Perspectives on the Tough Issues.* Nashville, TN: Abingdon Press, 2005.

Hamilton, Adam. *Seeing Gray in a World of Black and White.* Nashville, TN: Abingdon Press, 2008.

Hays, Richard B. "The Biblical Witness Concerning Homosexuality." In *Staying the Course,* edited by Maxie D. Dunnam and H. Newton Malony, 65-84. Nashville, TN: Abingdon Press, 2003.

Hinson, Bill. "Is It Time for an Amicable and Just Separation?" *Good News Magazine*, May 6, 2004. https://goodnewsmag.org/2015/01/is-it-time-for-an-amicable-and-just-separation/.

"John Wesley." Wikisource. https://en.wikisource.org/wiki/Author:John_Wesley.

Johnson, Luke Timothy. "Homosexuality & the Church." *Commonweal Magazine*, June 15, 2007. https://commonwealmagazine.org/homosexuality-church-1.

Lawrence, William B. and Sally Curtis AsKew. "Constitutional Methodism in Crisis: Historical and Operational Perspectives on Divisions Threatening United Methodism." *Methodist Review* 10 (2018): 23–72.

McCarthy, Justin. "Two in Three Americans Support Same-Sex Marriage." *Gallup*. May 23, 2018. https://news.gallup.com/poll/234866/two-three-americans-support-sex-marriage.aspx.

McDonald, Susan. "Lesbian No More." In *Staying the Course*, edited by Maxie D. Dunnam and H. Newton Malony, 170-174. Nashville, TN: Abingdon Press, 2003.

McNeill, John J. *Church and the Homosexual*, 4th ed. Boston, Massachusetts: Beacon Press, 1993.

"The Memphis Declaration." *UMCPage.org*. n.d. https://ucmpage.org/news/anti_evangelical_book3.html#The%20Memphis%20Declaration.

"A Message to The United Methodist Church." *Western Jurisdiction of the United Methodist Church*. March 14, 2017. http://westernjurisdictionumc.org/a-message-to-the-united-methodist-church/.

No Such Law. Reconciling Ministries Network. n.d. http://www.rmnetwork.org/newrmn/wp-content/uploads/2017/03/nosuchlawtoolkit.pdf?mc_cid=b40578ee68&mc_eid=d188497e99.

Oden, Thomas C. "The Classic Christian Exegesis on Romans 1:22-28." In *Staying the Course*, edited by Maxie D. Dunnam and H. Newton Malony, 85-96. Nashville, TN: Abingdon Press, 2003.

Oliveto, Karen P. *Our Strangely Warmed Hearts: Coming Out into God's Call*. Nashville, TN: Abingdon Press, 2018.

Ough, Bruce. "The Commission on a Way Forward" Public Letter. http://s3.amazonaws.com/Website_Properties/news-media/press-center/documents/The_Commission_On_A_Way_Forward.pdf.

Palmer, Gregory V. "Enforce." In *Finding Our Way*, edited by Rueben P. Job and Neil M. Alexander, 9-17. Nashville, TN: Abingdon Press, 2014.

Parr, Lois McCullen. "Bishop Talbert: A Call for Biblical Obedience." *Reconciling Ministries Network.* May 6, 2012. https://rmnetwork.org/gc-2012-altar-for-all/.

"Petitions." *Wesleyan Covenant Association.* n.d. https://wesleyancovenant.org/petitions/.

Plass, Ewald Martin. *What Luther Says: An Anthology, Volume 1.* St. Louis, MO: Concordia Publishing House, 1959.

Preusch, Matthew and Laurie Goodstein. "Jury of Methodists Clears Gay Minister Over a Relationship." *New York Times,* March 21, 2004. https://www.nytimes.com /2004/03/21/us/jury-of-methodists-clears-gay-minister-over-a-relationship.html.

Renfroe, Rob. "The DeLong Challenge." *Good News Magazine,* July 22, 2011. https://goodnewsmag.org/2011/07/the-delong-challenge/.

Renfroe, Rob and Walter Fenton. *Are We Really Better Together? An Evangelical Perspective on the Division in the UMC.* Nashville, TN: Abingdon Press, 2018.

"A Simple Plan." *UM Queer Clergy Caucus.* n.d. https://www.umqcc.org/a-simple-plan/.

Snyder, Howard A. *Homosexuality and the Church: Guidance for Community Conversation.* Franklin, TN: Seedbed Publishing, 2014.

Steinwert, Tiffany L. "Homosexuality and the United Methodist Church: An Ecclesiological Dilemma." PhD dissertation, Boston University, 2009.

Talbert, Melvin G. "Disobey." In *Finding Our Way,* edited by Rueben P. Job and Neil M. Alexander, 33-51. Nashville, TN: Abingdon Press, 2014.

Thorsen, Donald A. D. "John Wesley, Revelation, and Homosexual Experience." *Good News Magazine,* April 28, 2016. https://goodnewsmag.org/2016/04/john-wesley-revelation-and-homosexual-experience/.

Todd, Julie. "On the Body Being Broken," *Love Prevails.* May 12, 2016. https://loveprevailsumc.com/2016/05/12/on-the-body-being-broken/.

"Trial Summary." *Kairos CoMotion.* n.d. http://www.kairoscomotion.org/trial-summary/.

Watson, Kevin. "Experience in the So-Called 'Wesleyan Quadrilateral.'" *Vital Piety.* May 13, 2013. https://vitalpiety.com/2013/05/13/experience-in-the-so-called-wesleyan-quadrilateral/.

Wesley, John. "John Wesley's Notes on the Bible." Wesley Center Online. http://wesley.nnu.edu/john-wesley/john-wesleys-notes-on-the-bible/.

Made in the USA
Middletown, DE
03 November 2018